# GREAT CATS

EVERYTHING YOU WANT TO KNOW ABOUT ALL THE CATS YOU EVER LOVED FROM BOOKS, MOVIES, TELEVISION, THE COMICS, AND REAL LIFE!

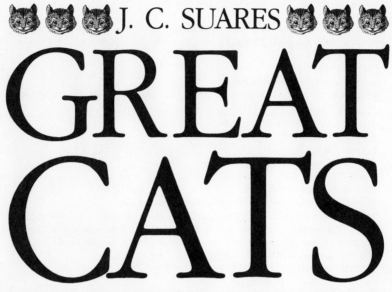

J. C. SUARES

# GREAT CATS

## THE WHO'S WHO OF FAMOUS FELINES

BANTAM BOOKS

TORONTO · NEW YORK · LONDON · SYDNEY

GREAT CATS: The Who's Who of Famous Felines
A Bantam Book/December 1981
(Note: Every effort has been made to locate the copyright owners of material
reproduced in this book. Omissions brought to our attention will be corrected in
subsequent editions.)

Library of Congress Cataloging in Publication Data
Suares, Jean-Claude.
    Great cats.
    1. Cats—Legends and stories.  I. Title.
SF445.5.S89          700          81-43099
ISBN 0-553-01338-6 (pbk.) AACR2
Published simultaneously in the United States and Canada.
Bantam Books are published by Bantam Books, Inc. Its trademark, consisting of the
words "Bantam Books" and the portrayal of a rooster, is Registered in U.S. Patent and
Trademark Office and in other countries. Marca Registrada. Bantam Books, Inc.,
666 Fifth Avenue, New York, New York 10103.
PRINTED IN THE UNITED STATES OF AMERICA

0 9 8 7 6 5 4 3 2 1

Research and permissions: Judith Linn
Production: Caroline Ginesi
Typesetting: Leland & Penn

Line drawings by J.C. Suares

DICK WHITTINGTON'S CAT
*His instinct for mousing made
his owner a wealthy man.*

# INTRODUCTION

COW
*Fat cat/television addict.*

"I'll tell you something interesting about cats," says Michael O'Donoghue, a full-time cat fancier also known to *Saturday Night Live* audiences as the macabre Mr. Mike. "Everybody thinks that *their* cats are the best. They don't feel that way about anything else—they don't think their wives or their cars or even their dogs are the best—but they all think their cats are just terrific. Amazing product, cats. And real simple to manufacture."

Naturally enough, Michael O'Donoghue thinks that *his* cats (including Cow, a hefty television addict listed herein) are better than anyone else's. And, just as naturally, we believe that *our* cats—the superior felines included in *Great Cats*—are the *crème de la crème,* the top of the heap. But we'll admit the possibility that in compiling this volume, we may have overlooked one or two prime examples more than worthy of inclusion in an opus like *Great Cats.* Perhaps even three or four.

The fact is that editors are subject to the same blind spots and prejudices that afflict all cat fanciers. Our greatest problem in creating *Great Cats* was not in deciding which cats to include but which we dared leave out (due to limitations of space). As a result, we may have omitted one of your favorite felines in our final selection. But we feel confident that all readers will find in these pages many delightful facts about the world's greatest cats.

KRAZY KAT
*George Herriman's classic cartoon kitty receives a love note from Ignatz Mouse.*

TWAIN'S CATS
*A small delegation from Mark Twain's large menagerie catnaps in a wicker chair on his front porch.*

**A**

## AESOP'S CATS, legendary figures.

Legend holds that Aesop was a freed slave who lived in Thrace five or six centuries before the birth of Christ, although most scholars believe that the fables attributed to him were the work of many hands.

### The Cat and Aphrodite

A cat fell in love with a handsome youth and begged Aphrodite to change her into a woman. The goddess, pitying her sad state, transformed her into a beautiful girl, and when the young man saw her he fell in love with her and took her home to be his wife. While they were resting in their bedroom, Aphrodite, who was curious to know if the cat's instincts had changed along with her shape, let a mouse loose in front of her. She at once forgot where she was, leapt up from the bed, and ran after the mouse to eat it. The indignant goddess then restored her to her original form.

*Moral:* A bad man retains his character even if his outward appearance is altered.

### The Cat and the Cock

A cat wanted to find a good excuse for killing and eating a cock which she had caught. She declared that he made himself a nuisance to men by crowing at night and preventing them from sleeping. The cock's defense was that he did men a good turn by waking them to start their day's work. Then the cat charged him with committing the unnatural sin of incest with his mother and sisters. The cock replied that this was also of use to his owners, because it made the hens lay well. "You are full of likely stories," said the cat, "but that is no reason why I should go hungry." So she made a meal of him.

*Moral:* An evil nature is bent on wrongdoing, with or without the cloak of a fair-sounding pretext.

### The Cat and the Fox

A fox was boasting to a cat one day about how clever he was. "Why, I have a whole bag of tricks," he bragged. "I know at least a hundred different ways of escaping my enemies, the dogs."

"How remarkable," said the cat. "I have only one trick, though I usually make it work. I wish you could teach me some of yours."

"Well, sometime when I have nothing else to do," said the fox, "I might teach you one or two of my easier ones."

Just at that moment they heard the yelping of a pack of hounds coming straight toward the spot where they stood. Quickly the cat scampered up a tree and disappeared in the leaves. "This is the trick I told you about," she called down to the fox. "Which one are you going to use?"

The fox sat there trying to decide which of his many tricks he was going to employ. Nearer and nearer came the hounds. When it was already too late, the fox decided to run for it. But even before he started, the dogs were upon him, and that was the end of the fox.

*Moral:* One good plan that works is better than a hundred doubtful ones.

THE CAT AND THE FOX

## The Cat and the Hens

A cat heard that there were some sick hens on a farm. So he disguised himself as a doctor and presented himself there, complete with medical bag. He stood outside the farmhouse and called to the hens to ask how they were. "Fine," came the reply—"if you will get off the premises."

*Moral:* A villain, try as he may to act like an honest man, cannot fool a man of sense.

## The Cat and the Mice

A house was overrun with mice. A cat who discovered this went there, and caught and ate them one by one. These constant attacks scared the survivors into their holes, where the cat could no longer get at them. So he decided that he must entice them out somehow. He climbed up the wall, hung himself on a peg, and played dead. But one of the mice, peeping out and seeing him, said: "It's no use, my friend; I'll keep out of your way, even if you do turn yourself into a sack."

*Moral:* Wise men learn by experience, and are never deceived by the false pretenses of an enemy.

*Aesop's Fables*

THE CAT AND THE MICE

**ANDY, pet and recordholder; belongs to Florida Senator Ken Myer; won a place in the record books when he fell from the sixteenth floor of a Miami apartment building and lived to meow about it; holds world record for longest fall by a living cat.**

**ARIEL, pet; orange Persian; belonged to Carl Van Vechten (1880-1964), author of *The Tiger in the House* (1920); see also FEATHERS.**

It is the popular belief that cats have an inherent dislike for water, and in general they are catabaptists, but my Ariel had no aversion to water; indeed, this orange Persian puss was accustomed to leap voluntarily into my warm morning tub, and she particularly liked to sit in the wash-hand-bowl under the open faucet.

> Carl Van Vechten
> *The Tiger in the House*

ARIEL

**ATOSSA, literary character; described on several occasions by English poet Matthew Arnold (1882-88).**

So Tiberius might have sat,
Had Tiberius been a cat.

> Matthew Arnold

# B

## BASTET, Egyptian cat goddess; symbolized femininity and maternity; flourished around 2000 B.C.

Suppose a cat died a natural death under a family roof. The inhabitants of the house shaved their eyebrows and lamented loudly for hours. The eyes of the beloved deceased were piously closed. The whiskers were firmly pressed down against its lips. And then it was wound round with a mummy's wrappings. According to the district of the country, precise rules governed the funeral laying out. In some places, fragments of painted cloth replaced the eyes, now forever closed. In others, two small artificial ears stood up from the head, giving an appearance of attentiveness to this now immobile face. Elsewhere, turquoise collars were wound round the neck of the sacred beast. Then came the embalming of the mummy. Depending on how rich its masters were, it was either buried or placed in a true sarcophagus. There is still one of these to be seen in the Cairo Museum.

Fernand Mery
*The Life, History and Magic of the Cat*

BASTET
*Worshipped by the Egyptians.*

## THE BLACK CAT, fictional character; named Pluto; black; created by American writer Edgar Allan Poe (1809-49); first appeared in story "The Black Cat" (1843).

Pluto, according to Poe's story, "was a remarkably large and beautiful animal, entirely black, and sagacious to an astonishing degree." It was also the cherished pet of the story's narrator, an ordinary married man who fed, protected, and amused it. Their relationship proceeds harmoniously until the man, seized by a fit of what he calls "perverseness," gradually comes to despise the animal. As the story moves toward its horrifying conclusion, readers may find themselves agreeing with the narrator's wife, who once suggested that Pluto, and all black cats, might be a witch in disguise.

Pluto is, among other things, a physical manifestation of the narrator's conscience. When the narrator descends into a life of drunkenness and debauchery, his affection for the cat disappears, and he is led first to maim and then murder it. With the death of the cat, the narrator's own final downfall begins, ending only after he has murdered his wife. During this part of the story, Pluto is present in the form of a nearly identical cat that is ultimately responsible for bringing the narrator to justice. This second

POE

*right:*
THE BLACK CAT
*Bela Lugosi is confronted by the shadow of his murdered pet in a scene from the famous 1930's movie version of Edgar Allan Poe's classic tale of horror.*

black cat has a single white marking that gradually develops into the clear outline of a gallows—precisely anticipating the fate of the narrator.

Pluto—this was the cat's name—was my favorite pet and playmate. I alone fed him, and he attended me wherever I went about the house. It was even with difficulty that I could prevent him from following me through the streets.

Our friendship lasted, in this manner, for several years, during which my general temperament and character—through the instrumentality of the Fiend Intemperance—had (I blush to confess it) experienced a radical alteration for the worse. I grew, day by day, more moody, more irritable, more regardless of the feeling of others. At length, I even offered her personal violence. My pets, of course, were made to feel the change in my disposition. I not only neglected, but ill-used them. For Pluto, however, I still retained sufficient regard to restrain me from maltreating him, as I made no scruple of maltreating the rabbits, the monkey, or even the dog, when by accident, or through affection, they came in my way. But my disease grew upon me—for what disease is like Alcohol!—and at length even Pluto, who was now becoming old, and consequently somewhat peevish—even Pluto began to experience the effects of my ill temper.

One night, returning home, much intoxicated, from one of my haunts about town, I fancied that the cat avoided my presence. I seized him; when, in his fright at my violence, he inflicted a slight wound upon my hand with his teeth. The fury of a demon instantly possessed me. I knew myself no longer. My original soul seemed, at once, to take its flight from my body; and a more than fiendish malevolence, gin-nurtured, thrilled every fibre of my frame. I took from my waistcoat-pocket a pen-knife, opened it, grasped the poor beast by the throat, and deliberately cut one of its eyes from the socket! I blush, I burn, I shudder, while I pen the damnable atrocity.

Edgar Allan Poe
"The Black Cat"

**BOOTH'S CATS, cartoon characters; created by George Booth (1926-    ); appear in Booth's frequent contributions to *The New Yorker* and other magazines, and also in several collections, including *Think Good Thoughts About a Pussy-Cat.***

I started drawing cats as a result of marrying into a cat-loving family. I

THE BLACK CAT
*Drawing by Aubrey Beardsley, the English illustrator, for an 1895 edition of Poe's story.*

*right:*
BOOTH'S CATS
*A recent* New Yorker *cartoon.*

*"Last night I heard a cicada."*

married twenty-two years ago and received a cat education from that point on. My wife's family had always had cats and always loved them. I had a cat myself when I was a kid—a sort of a wild cat. I grew up in the Midwest, and cats out there are pretty wild.

I observe cats a lot and do sketches of them, and I arrive at my drawings that way. I have a cat now who thinks he's a dog—you can see it in the way he sits, the way he thinks—but that's all right with me. We have two cats: Ambrosia and James Taylor. We got them as kittens from a girl who was giving them away in front of a supermarket, and as time went by we found out that James Taylor was a girl and Ambrosia was a boy. So now we call them Amberson and Tata. Amberson is the one who thinks he's a dog. He doesn't bark, though; he just purrs.

George Booth
*Creator*

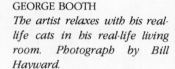

**BROBDINGNAGIAN CAT, fictional character; nameless; created by Irish satirist Jonathan Swift (1667–1745); first appeared in *Gulliver's Travels* (1726).**

The Brobdingnagian cat is an animal of enormous size encountered by Lemuel Gulliver in Part II of Swift's satiric classic. The cat's home is

Brobdingnag, a mysterious island visited by Gulliver after his safe return from Lilliput at the end of Part I. In contrast to Lilliput, where none of the inhabitants stood more than six inches tall, Brobdingnag is a land of giants. The grass grows twenty feet high, the men are the size of trees, and the cats are larger than oxen. This particular cat belongs to the farmer who captures Gulliver immediately after his arrival. Gulliver first meets the cat at dinner time in the farmer's house.

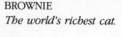

BROWNIE
*The world's richest cat.*

In the midst of dinner, my mistress's favorite cat leaped into her lap. I heard a noise behind me like that of a dozen stocking weavers at work. Turning my head, I found it proceeded from the purring of this animal, who seemed to be three times larger than an ox, as I computed by the view of her head, and one of her paws, while her mistress was feeding and stroking her. The fierceness of this creature's countenance altogether discomposed me; though I stood at the farther end of the table, above fifty feet off, and although my mistress held her fast for fear she might give a spring and seize me in her talons. But it happened there was no danger; for the cat took not the least notice of me when my master placed me within three yards of her. And as I have been always told, and found true by experience in my travels, that flying or displaying fear before a fierce animal is a certain way to make it pursue or attack you, so I resolved in this dangerous juncture to show no manner of concern. I walked with intrepidity five or six times before the very head of the cat, and came within half a yard of her; whereupon she drew herself back, as if she were more afraid of me.

Jonathan Swift
*Gulliver's Travels*

**BROOMSTICKS, see SAM**

**BROWNIE and HELLCAT, pets and recordholders; belonged to Dr. William Grier of San Diego, Calif.; richest cats on record; inherited $415,000 when owner died in 1963; money went to George Washington University, Washington, D.C., when cats died two years later.**

# C

**CALVIN, pet; Angora; belonged to American writer Charles Dudley Warner (1829–1900).**

CALVIN

Calvin was Warner's prize pet. When Calvin died, Warner wrote, "I had only one cat, and he was more a companion than a cat. When he departed this life I did not care to, as many men do when their partners die, take a second."

The intelligence of Calvin was something phenomenal, in his rank of life. He established a method of communicating his wants, and even some of his sentiments; and he could help himself in many things. There was a furnace register in a retired room, where he used to go when he wished to be alone, that he always opened when he desired more heat; but never shut it, any more than he shut the door after himself. . . . I hesitate a little to speak of his capacity for friendship and the affectionateness of his nature, for I know from his own reserve that he would not care to have it much talked about. We understood each other perfectly, but we never made any fuss about it; when I spoke his name and snapped my fingers, he came to me; when I returned home at night, he was pretty sure to be waiting for me near the gate, and would rise and saunter along the walk, as if his being there was purely accidental—so shy was he commonly of showing feeling. There was one thing he never did—he never rushed through an open doorway. He never forgot his dignity. If he had asked to have the door opened, and was eager to go out, he always went out deliberately; I can see him now, standing on the sill, looking about at the sky as if he was thinking whether it were worthwhile to take an umbrella, until he was near having his tail shut in.

Charles Dudley Warner

**THE CAT, fictional character; created by C. Collodi (pseudonym of Carlo Lorenzini); first appeared in *The Adventures of Pinocchio* (1883).**

The Cat in *The Adventures of Pinocchio* is the evil accomplice of the equally evil Fox, the two of whom conspire to cheat Pinocchio out of five gold pieces he has been given by a puppeteer who feels sorry for him. The Cat, disguised as a blind beggar, and the Fox, pretending to be lame, first encounter the innocent and unwary Pinocchio on a country road. They promise to help him turn his coins into a large fortune, telling him that if he plants them in the ground at a certain place, they will sprout into gold trees bearing coins instead of leaves. Their only object, of course, is to rob him, and after they have succeeded in doing so, they disappear. Pinocchio doesn't encounter them again until near the end of his adventures as he and Gepetto, his wood-carving foster father, are walking along a road:

They had not taken a hundred steps when they saw two rough-looking individuals sitting on a stone begging for alms.

It was the Fox and the Cat, but one could hardly recognize them, they looked so miserable. The Cat, after pretending to be blind for so many years, had really lost the sight of both eyes. And the Fox, old, thin, and almost hairless, had even lost his tail. That sly thief had fallen into deepest poverty, and one day he had been forced to sell his beautiful tail for a bite to eat.

"Oh, Pinocchio," he cried in a tearful voice. "Give us some alms, we beg of you! We are old, tired, and sick."

"Sick!" repeated the Cat.

"Addio, false friends!" answered the Marionette. "You cheated me once, but you will never catch me again."

"Believe us! Today we are truly poor and starving."

"Starving!" repeated the Cat.

"If you are poor, you deserve it! Remember the old proverb which says: 'Stolen money never bears fruit.' Addio, false friends!"

> C. Collodi
> *The Adventures of Pinocchio*

## THE CAT IN THE HAT, fictional character; created by Dr. Seuss; first appeared in *The Cat in the Hat* (1957).

The Cat in the Hat is a mysterious, magical creature in a top hat who entertains two bored children one day while their mother is away from the house. The Cat's antics alarm the children and their pet goldfish, all of whom are worried that the cat will make such a mess of the house that the mother will be furious and scold them. Furniture flies in every direction, the goldfish is juggled in his bowl, vases sail through the air. But just when it seems certain that disaster is inevitable, the Cat produces a fabulous machine that whisks through the house and returns everything to its proper order. When the mother returns, she has no idea that her home has been the scene of a three-ring circus.

"Look at me!
Look at me now!" said the Cat.

THE CAT IN THE HAT
*One-cat home entertainment.*

"With a cup and a cake
On the top of my hat!
I can hold up TWO books!
I can hold up the fish!
And a little toy ship!
And some milk on a dish!
And look!
I can hop up and down on the ball!
But that is not all!
Oh, no,
That is not all..."

## THE CAT THAT WALKED BY HIMSELF, fictional character; created by Rudyard Kipling (1865-1936); first appeared in *The Just So Stories* (1902).

Kipling's story of "The Cat That Walked by Himself" is a lighthearted mythic explanation for certain aspects of the modern house cat's personality, in particular its legendary independence. The Cat in the story is the last of the creatures of the Wild Wet Wood to sacrifice a measure of its wildness in return for the care and protection of men, the new species on the block. After all of the other animals in the wood—the Dog, the Horse, and the Cow—have won themselves places in the world of humans by agreeing to serve or befriend them, the Cat makes an appearance at the humans' cave and says, "I am not a friend, and I am not a servant. I am the Cat who walks by himself and I wish to come into your cave." The woman is unimpressed and tells him to go away, but she promises, at the Cat's urging, to reconsider his banishment if he manages to earn her praise on three separate occasions. This he eventually manages to do, twice by soothing the woman's baby and once by catching a mouse. All that remains for him to do is come to some kind of agreement with the Man and his Dog, who weren't in on the original bargain:

That evening when the Man and the Dog came into the Cave, the Woman told them all the story of the bargain, while the Cat sat by the fire and smiled. Then the Man said, "Yes, but he has not made a bargain with *me* or with all proper Men after me." Then he took off his two leather boots and he took up his little stone axe (that makes three) and he fetched a piece of wood and a hatchet (that is five altogether), and he set them out in a row and he said, "Now we will make *our* bargain. If

KIPLING

you do not catch mice when you in the Cave for always and always and always, I will throw these five things at you whenever I see you, and so shall all proper Men do after me."

"Ah!" said the Woman, listening. "This is a very clever Cat, but he is not so clever as my Man."

The Cat counted the five things (and they looked very knobby) and he said, "I will catch mice when I am in the Cave for always and always and always; but *still* I am the Cat who walks by himself, and all places are alike to me."

"Not when I am near," said the Man. "If you had not said that last I would have put all these things away for always and always and always; but now I am going to throw my two boots and my little stone axe (that makes three) at you whenever I meet you. And so shall all proper Men do after me!"

Then the Dog said, "Wait a minute. He has not made a bargain with *me* or with all proper Dogs after me." And he showed his teeth and said, "If you are not kind to the Baby while I am in the Cave for always and always and always, I will hunt you till I catch you, and when I catch you I will bite you. And so shall all proper Dogs after me."

"Ah!" said the Woman, listening. "This is a very clever Cat, but he is not so clever as the Dog."

The Cat counted the Dog's teeth (and they looked very pointed) and he said, "I will be kind to the Baby while I am in the Cave, as long as he does not pull my tail too hard, for always and always and always. But *still* I am the Cat who walks by himself, and all places are alike to me."

"Not when I am near," said the Dog. "If you had not said that last I would have shut my mouth for always and always and always; but *now* I am going to hunt you up a tree whenever I meet you. And so shall all proper Dogs do after me."

Then the Man threw his two boots and his little stone axe (that makes three) at the Cat, and the Cat ran out of the Cave and the Dog chased him up a tree; and from that day to this, Best Beloved, three proper Men out of five will always throw things at a Cat whenever they meet him, and all proper Dogs will chase him up a tree. But the Cat keeps his side of the bargain too. He will kill mice, and he will be kind to Babies when he is in the house, just as long as they do not pull his tail too hard. But when he has done that, and between times, and when the moon gets up and night comes, he is the Cat that walks by himself, and all places are alike to him. Then he goes out to the Wet Wild Woods or up the Wet

Wild Trees or on the Wet Wild Roofs, waving his wild tail and walking by his wild lone."

Rudyard Kipling
"The Cat That Walked By Himself"

**CATASAUQUA, fictional character; Manx; created by Mark Twain (pseudonym of Samuel Langhorne Clemens, 1835-1910); first appeared in *Letters from the Earth* (1962); mother of kittens Cattaraugus (white) and Cataline (black); see also TWAIN'S CATS and TOM QUARTZ.**

CATASAUQUA

Twain introduced Catasauqua *et al.* in a hilarious bedtime tale he used to tell his young daughters. "They think my tales are better than paregoric, and quicker," Twain explained. "While I talk, they make comments and ask questions, and we have a pretty good time." Twain's tale is too long to reproduce in its entirety, but the opening paragraphs are printed below.

Once there was a noble big cat, whose Christian name was Catasauqua—because she lived in that region—but she did not have any surname, because she was a short-tailed cat—being a Manx—and did not need one. It is very just and becoming in a long-tailed cat to have a surname, but it would be very ostentatious, and even dishonorable, in a Manx. Well, Catasauqua had a beautiful family of catlings; and they were of different colors, to harmonize with their characters. Cattaraugus, the eldest, was white, and he had high impulses and a pure heart; Cataline, the youngest, was black, and he had a self-seeking nature, his motives were nearly always base, he was truculent and insincere. He was vain and foolish, and often said he would rather be what he was, and live like a bandit, yet have none above him, than be a cat-o'-nine-tails and eat with the King. He hated his harmless and unoffending little catercousins, and frequently drove them from his presence with imprecations, and at times even resorted to violence.

SUSY: What are catercousins, Papa?

Quarter-cousins—it is so set down in the big dictionary. You observe I refer to it every now and then. This is because I do not wish to make any mistakes, my purpose being to instruct as well as entertain. Whenever I use a word which you do not understand, speak up and I will look and find out what it means. But do not interrupt me except for cause, for I am always excited when I am erecting history, and want to get on. Well, one day Catasauqua met with misfortune; her house burned down. It was the very day after it had been insured for double its value, too—how singular! Yes, and how lucky! This often happens. It teaches us that mere loading a house down with insurance isn't going to save it. Very well, Catasauqua took the insurance money and built a new house; and a much better one, too; and what is more, she had money left to add a gaudy concatenation of extra improvements with. Oh, I tell you! What she didn't know about catallactics no other cat need ever try to acquire.

CLARA: What is catallactics, Papa?

The dictionary intimates, in a nebulous way, that it is a sort of demi-synonym for the science commonly called political economy.

CLARA: Thank you, Papa.

> Mark Twain
> "A Cat's Tail"

**CHESHIRE CAT, fictional character; created by Lewis Carroll (pseudonym of Charles Lutwidge Dodgson, 1832-98); illustrated by Sir John Tenniel (1820-1914) and others; chiefly noted for its grin, paradoxical speech, and ability to vanish into thin air.**

The Cheshire Cat is the enigmatic grinning cat who appears (and disappears) in *Alice's Adventures in Wonderland,* Lewis Carroll's classic children's book first published in 1865. The Cat takes its name from an old English folk saying in which a person is said to "grin like a Cheshire cat." The origin of this folk saying, according to Martin Gardner in *The Annotated Alice* (New York, 1960), is uncertain, but it may refer back to certain Cheshire cheeses, which were once molded in the shape of grinning cats.

Alice first runs into the Cheshire Cat in the kitchen of the Duchess. When she later chastises the cat for "appearing and vanishing so suddenly," the Cat apologizes and then vanishes *slowly,* "beginning with the end of the tail, and ending with the grin, which remained some time after the rest of it had gone."

The Cat only grinned when it saw Alice. It looked good-natured, she thought: still it had *very* long claws and a great many teeth, so she felt that it ought to be treated with respect.

*"We're all mad here."*

"Cheshire Puss," she began, rather timidly, as she did not at all know whether it would like the name: however, it only grinned a little wider. "Come, it's pleased so far," thought Alice, and she went on. "Would you tell me, please, which way I ought to go from here?"

"That depends a good deal on where you want to go," said the Cat.

"I don't much care where—" said Alice.

"Then it doesn't matter which way you go," said the Cat.

"—so long as I get *somewhere,*" Alice added as an explanation.

"Oh, you're sure to do that," said the Cat, "if you only walk long enough."

Alice felt that this could not be denied, so she tried another question. "What sort of people live about here?"

"In *that* direction," the Cat said, waving its right paw round, "lives a Hatter: and in *that* direction," waving the other paw, "lives a March Hare. Visit either you like: they're both mad."

"But I don't want to go among mad people," Alice remarked.

"Oh, you can't help that," said the Cat. "We're all mad here. I'm mad. You're mad."

"How do you know I'm mad?" said Alice.

"You must be," said the Cat, "or you wouldn't have come here."

Lewis Carroll
*Alice's Adventures in Wonderland*

CHESSIE
*Making a friend in the galley of the dining car.*

**CHESSIE, fictional character and company mascot; created in 1934 by artist C. Gruenwald as a promotion for the Chesapeake & Ohio Railway; has appeared in numerous advertisements, brochures, calendars, and a book for children.**

When the kitten wasn't expecting it, a curtain brushed against her head. It seemed to dare her to grab it. She crouched and jumped and caught it. It moved again, and what do you suppose she saw above her? Five small pink toes sticking out between the curtains of the lower berth! She wanted to play with the toes so she scrambled up, digging her claws into the cloth. But, before she could even touch those little pink things, they were gone.

She peeked between the curtains, trying to find the toes, and there was the little boy they belonged to, lying in the berth. His left arm was wrapped in bandages. That was because he had broken it while he and

*Symbol of the Chesapeake and Ohio Railway.*

Two-footed Ones, He and She, have they alone the right to be sad, to be gay, to lick the plates, to complain, to be capricious? I too have *my* caprices, *my* griefs, *my* irregular appetites, *my* hours of dreamy retreat in which I withdraw from the world." Other of Colette's cats—whether real, fictional, or both—included Franchette, Saha, Zwerg, and La Chatte Derniere. When La Chatte Derniere died in 1939, Colette was so shaken that she vowed never to replace it and so was catless for the rest of her life.

He carried Saha alive in his arms. He went straight to the bedroom, pushed aside the things on the invisible dressing-table and gently put the cat on the slab of glass. She held herself upright and firm on her paws but her deep-set eyes wandered all about her as they would have done in a strange house.

"Saha!" called Alain in a whisper. "If there's nothing the matter with her, it's a miracle. Saha!"

She raised her head, as if to reassure her friend, and leant her cheek against his hand.

"Walk a little, Saha. Look, she's walking! Good Lord! Falling six storeys! It was the awning of the chap on the second floor that broke the fall. From there she bounced off on to the concierge's little lawn—the concierge saw her pass in the air. He said: 'I thought it was an umbrella falling.' What's she got on her ear? No, it's some white off the wall. Wait till I listen to her heart."

He laid the cat on her side and listened to the beating ribs, the tiny disordered mechanism. With his fair hair spread out and his eyes closed, he seemed to be sleeping on Saha's flank and to wake with a sigh only to see Camille standing there silent and apart, watching the close-knit group they made.

"Can you believe it? There's nothing wrong. At least I can't find anything wrong with her except a terribly agitated heart. But a cat's heart is usually agitated. But however could it have happened! I'm asking you if you could possibly know, my poor pet! She fell from this side," he said, looking at the open french window. "Jump down on the ground, Saha, if you can."

Colette
*La Chatte*

**COURAGEOUS CAT, animated-cartoon character; created in 1961 by Bob Kane; survived 130 television episodes.**

Courageous Cat and his fearless sidekick, Minute Mouse, were known as the "Masked Crusaders for Justice" in their native Empire City. Operating out of a fortress-like Cat Cave, the duo raced from crime to crime in their super-charged Cat Mobile and snared dangerous hoodlums with the Thousand-Purpose Cat Gun. Their numerous enemies included The Frog and Harry the Gorilla.

**COW, pet; black and white American shorthair; belongs to Michael O'Donoghue, former *Saturday Night Live* writer and star; weighs twenty-five pounds; likes to sit in the bathroom sink.**

> Cow is a television addict.
> Bill Hayward
> *Photographer*

COW
*Photograph by Bill Hayward.*

**THE CROOKED CAT, from a Mother Goose rhyme.**

> There was a crooked man,
>    and he walked a crooked mile,
> He found a crooked sixpence
>    Against a crooked stile;
> He bought a crooked cat,
>    Which caught a crooked mouse,
> And they all lived together
>    In a little crooked house.

CROOKED CAT

# D

**DICK WHITTINGTON'S CAT, fictional (?) character; legendary pet of Richard Whittington (? –1423), man of modest background who became mayor of London in 1397; subject of numerous versions of a folk tale in which the cat enables Whittington to become a wealthy, successful man.**

According to the legend, young Dick Whittington set out for London as a boy, hoping to make his fortune in the city whose streets, he had been told, were paved with gold. He found London to be considerably less magnificent than he had expected, and he nearly starved to death before a merchant named Fitzwarren hired him and put him to work in his kitchen. Because Whittington's room in Fitzwarren's house was infested with mice and rats, he bought a cat for a penny from a little girl on the street. Whittington and his cat lived happily together until Mr. Fitzwarren suggested that he "invest" the animal in a trading voyage he was sponsoring. Whittington despaired of parting with his treasured pet, but he was finally persuaded to. During the voyage, the cat proved itself to be such an adept mouser that it sold for ten times as much as the rest of the cargo put together. Whittington's windfall enabled him to marry Fitzwarren's daughter Alice, and eventually become mayor.

DICK WHITTINGTON'S CAT
*Title page illustration from an Aldermary Church Yard chapbook.*

The King and Queen were seated at the upper end of the room, and a number of dishes were brought in for dinner. They had not sat long when a vast number of rats and mice rushed in, helping themselves from almost every dish. The captain wondered at this, and asked if these vermin were not very unpleasant.

"Oh, yes," said they, "very destructive; and the King would give half his treasure to be freed of them, for they not only destroy his dinner, as you see, but they assault him in his chamber, and even in bed, so that he is obliged to be watched while he is sleeping for fear of them."

The captain jumped for joy; he remembered poor Whittington and his cat, and told the King that he had a creature on board the ship that would dispatch all these vermin immediately. The King's heart leapt so high at the happiness this news gave hime that his turban dropped off his head. "Bring this creature to me," said he; "vermin are dreadful in a Court, and if she will perform what you say I will load your ship with gold and jewels in exchange for her."

The captain, who knew his business, took this opportunity to set forth the merits of Mrs. Puss. He told His Majesty that it would be inconvenient to part with her, as, when she was gone, the rats and mice might destroy the goods in the ship—but to oblige His Majesty he would fetch her.

"Run, run!" said the Queen; "I am impatient to see the dear creature."

Away went the captain to the ship, while another dinner was got ready. He put Puss under his arm, and arrived at the place soon enough to see the table full of rats.

When the cat saw them she did not wait for bidding, but jumped out of the captain's arms, and in a few minutes laid almost all the rats and

mice dead at her feet. The rest of them in their fright scampered away to their holes.

The King and Queen were quite charmed to get so easily rid of such plagues, and desired the creature who had done them so great a kindness might be brought to them for inspection. Upon which the captain called: "Pussy, pussy, pussy!" and she came to him. He then presented her to the Queen, who started back, and was afraid to touch a creature who had made such a havoc among the rats and mice. However, when the captain stroked the cat and called "Pussy, pussy," the Queen also touched her and cried "Putty, putty," for she had not learned English. He then put her down on the Queen's lap, where she, purring, played with Her Majesty's hand, and then sung herself to sleep.

The King, having seen the exploits of Mrs. Puss, and being informed that her kittens would stock the whole country, bargained with the captain for the whole ship's cargo, and then gave him ten times as much for the cat as all the rest amounted to.

*Dick Whittington's Cat*

## DINAH, fictional character; created by Lewis Carroll (pseudonym of Charles Lutwidge Dodgson, 1832–98).

Dinah is Alice's pet cat. She makes cameo appearances in both *Alice's Adventures in Wonderland,* which was first published in 1865, and in *Through the Looking-Glass,* which was published seven years later. Dinah was named after a real cat owned by Lorina, Alice, and Edith Liddell, Carroll's "three little maidens," whom he met on July 4, 1862 and who (in particular, Alice) inspired his stories. Dinah's role in *Wonderland* is fleeting, but in *Through the Looking-Glass,* she and her kittens set the story in motion. Her kittens are Kitty (who is black) and Snowdrop (who is white).

The way Dinah washed her children's faces was this: first she held the poor thing down by its ears with one paw, and then with the other paw she rubbed its face all over, the wrong way, beginning at the nose: and just now, as I said, she was hard at work on the white kitten, which was lying quite still and trying to purr—no doubt feeling that it was all meant for its good.

But the black kitten had been finished with earlier in the afternoon, and so, while Alice was sitting curled up in a corner of the great armchair, half talking to herself and half asleep, the kitten had been having a grand game of romps with the ball of worsted Alice had been trying to wind up, and had been rolling it up and down till it had all come undone again; and there it was, spread over the hearth-rug, all knots and tangles, with the kitten running after its own tail in the middle.

"Oh, you wicked little thing!" cried Alice, catching up the kitten, and giving it a little kiss to make it understand that it was in disgrace. "Really, Dinah ought to have taught you better manners! You *ought,* Dinah, you know you ought!"

Lewis Carroll
*Through the Looking-Glass*

DINAH
*Alice's pet. Drawings by John Tenniel.*

# E

## DUSTY, pet and recordholder; home, Bonham, Texas; most prolific cat on record; gave birth to 420 kittens, the last on June 12, 1952.

## ESMERALDA, comic-strip character; black stripes; created by Al Smith (1902–    ); first appeared in strip called "Cicero's Cat," December 3, 1933.

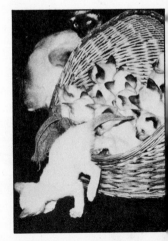

DUSTY
*Four hundred and twenty times a mother.*

# F

**FEATHERS, pet; tortoise-shell-and-white smoke tabby Persian; belonged to Carl Van Vechten (1880–1964), author of _The Tiger in the House_ (1920); see also ARIEL.**

She wants her breakfast at a certain hour in the morning; if the door of my bedroom is closed she gives little cries outside. If it is open she enters, puts her forepaws on the edge of my bed close to my face and licks my cheek. If I brush her away, in a few moments she is nibbling my toes. I put an end to this and very shortly she is marching up and down, using me as a highroad. She is equally persistent if I am taking a nap. On such occasions she often climbs high on my breast and sleeps with me, but when she awakes she digs her claws into my chest and stretches, quite as if I didn't exist. This alternate protrusion of the forepaws, with toes separated, as if pushing against and sucking their mother's teats, is a favourite gesture of cats when they are pleased.

Carl Van Vechten
_The Tiger in the House_

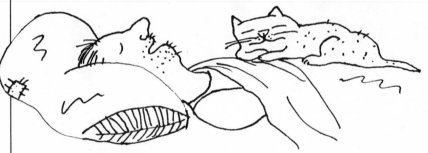

FEATHERS

**FELIX THE CAT, animated-cartoon and comic-strip character; created in 1917 in animated short film by Australian-born American cartoonist Pat Sullivan 1887–1933).**

Krazy Kat may be the greatest cartoon cat of all time, but Felix is probably the most popular. Making his first appearance in 1917, Felix was an immediate hit with audiences all over this country and, eventually, the world. In the decades that have followed, Felix has changed somewhat in form and personality, but he's still very much with us, and a revival of his popular television cartoon series is currently in the works.

Young fans might not recognize the original Felix, who had no bag of

tricks (a gimmick invented for television) and no magical powers. But even unadorned, Felix was immensely popular, appearing in more than a hundred animated films in the sixteen years between his debut and his creator's death. He was the star of the first cartoon "talkie" ever made, beating Walt Disney's Mickey Mouse (a character very definitely derived from Felix) by a full year. He was also the star of one of the first television broadcasts ever made; when NBC was making its first experiments with television transmission in 1928, Felix was the image that appeared on the screen. NBC's engineers couldn't find human volunteers to stand under the hot lights while they tinkered with their cameras, so a twelve-inch statuette of Felix was recruited instead. The statuette was placed on a small turntable and made to rotate in front of the cameras for hours on end. The cameramen and engineers grew so fond of Felix that they were reluctant to abandon him; he remained NBC's "test pattern" until the late 1930's.

In addition to his movie and television career, Felix was a popular figure in newspapers and comic books. His Sunday comic-strip debut was on August 14, 1923, with the King Features Syndicate, and his daily-strip debut was May 9, 1927. He also made numerous comic-book appearances in *Popular Comics* and *Toby Comics*. Although Felix has stepped out of the limelight for the moment, his producer is planning a full-scale comeback for the near future.

Felix is not just a cat, he is the cat. I would like to say that he is a super-cat, because he belongs to no category of the animal kingdom. At times he imitates the gestures of the humans among whom he finds himself, but he does not stay with them. With a bound, he reaches the realms of fantasy and installs himself there. . . .

He has escaped the reality of the cat; he is made up of an extraordinary personality. When he is walking like a man preoccupied, with his head buried in his shoulders, his paws behind his back, he becomes the impossible in cats, the unreal in men.

He is honest, generous, fearless, and optimistic. He is ingenious and fertile in resourcefulness. Nothing is more familiar to him than the extraordinary, and when he is not surrounded by the fantastic, he creates it.

And it is this creative faculty which quite richly holds us in Felix. It arises from two mental attitudes: astonishment and curiosity. The virtues of poets and scholars. His familarity with the exceptional has not deprived him of that admirable quality: the capacity to marvel. Felix constructs a universe using only two properties, both originating

in him, material signs of the state of his own soul: the exclamation mark and the question mark. Nothing more is needed for building a world!
Marcel Brion

**FIGARO, animated-cartoon character; pet belonging to woodcarver Gepetto in Walt Disney's full-length cartoon, *The Adventures of Pinocchio*.**

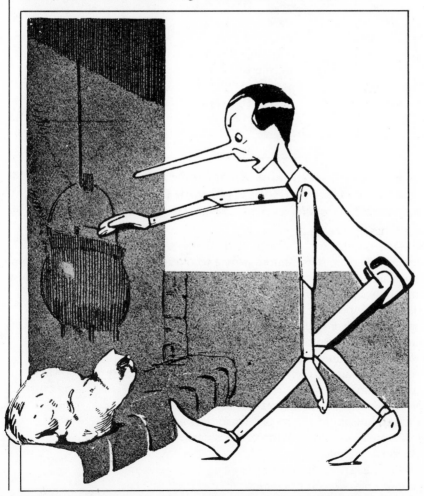

FIGARO
*Gepetto's cat.*

**FOSS**, pet; belonged to Edward Lear (1812–88), author of "The Owl and the Pussy-cat"; depicted in many humorous drawings by the author; see also PUSSY-CAT.

FOSS
*Edward Lear's drawing of himself and his cat.*

**FRITZ THE CAT**, comic-strip and animated-cartoon character; created by artist R. [Robert] Crumb (1943–19  ); first appeared in strip called "Fred the Teenage Girl Pigeon" (1965).

Fritz is probably the best-known character in R. Crumb's teeming pantheon of underground-comic stars. Almost anyone who was alive in the sixties remembers him either from his occasional appearances in the underground comic books of the day or from books like *Head Comix* (New York, 1968), which helped give Fritz (and Crumb) a truly national audience. Fritz reached the silver screen, amid great controversy, in 1972 in an X-rated animated extravaganza by Ralph Bakshi, the rising Walt Disney of the underground. Crumb was so upset by the film that he first tried to block its release in court and then drew a "farewell" strip in which Fritz was murdered by an ostrich.

Fritz the Cat is essentially a phony, and the fact that he is a cat is arbitrary. He is quite human, in fact more human than many of the people Crumb was to draw later in his career. He is a con-man, a sex maniac, and totally incorrigible.

Joe Brancatelli
*The World Encyclopedia of Comics*

FRITZ THE CAT
*In his own comic book (above) and his own movie (right).*

# G

**GARFIELD, comic-strip character; orange tiger; created in 1978 by Jim Davis (1945- ); named after artist's grandfather; appears in approximately seven hundred newspapers; subject of best-selling books *Garfield at Large* (New York, 1980) and *Garfield Gains Weight* (New York, 1981); characteristic saying, "Show me a good mouser and I'll show you a cat with bad breath."**

Garfield has been described by his fictional owner, cartoonist Jon Arbuckle, as "a lasagna with fur and fangs," and most of his fans would have to agree. Garfield is a compact cartoon terror who simultaneously drives his owner crazy and keeps his millions of admirers in stitches. He hangs from the ceiling, smokes pipes, drinks coffee, eats olives, and conducts a running war with a not-too-bright dog named Odie. Garfield also hates cat food ("the bouquet leaves something to be desired"), likes goldfish ("call it an ethnic weakness"), loves lasagna ("nature's most perfect food"), dislikes television commercials ("they're too short for a trip to the sandbox") can't help playing with Jon Arbuckle's chicken soup ("the devil made me do it"), abhors diets ("when the lasagna content in my blood gets low, I get mean"), eats wax fruit ("everything tastes good when you're on a diet"), and detests dogs ("They're rusting our nation's fire hydants").

He is, in a word, a person.

"Garfield," says Jon Arbuckle in one of Davis's strips, "you sleep too much, you eat too much, and you watch too much television."

"What does Jon expect of me, anyway?" Garfield replies. "I'm only human."

One reason Garfield is interesting for cat lovers is that he confirms what they've always suspected about cats. In Garfield they see his human aspects—his refusal to diet, his inability to walk through a room without knocking things over, and his total pursuit of warm places to curl up and sleep. He champions a lot of unpopular causes, like anti-jogging, and what's more, he doesn't apologize for them.

Jim Davis
Interview in *People* Magazine

GARFIELD
*"When the lasagna content in my blood gets low, I get mean."*

PUSH

SLURP!

SCRATCH
SCRATCH
SCRATCH
SCRATCH
SCRATCH

GARFIELD Characters: © 1978
United Feature Syndicate, Inc.

© 1979 United Feature Syndicate, Inc.

JIM DAVIS

7-8

**GINGER, fictional character; yellow tom; created by Beatrix Potter (1866-1943); first appeared in *Ginger and Pickles* (1909), written and illustrated by Miss Potter; see also SIMPKIN and TOM KITTEN.**

Ginger, in Miss Potter's story, is an enterprising feline who owns a small village shop in partnership with a dog named Pickles. In their business, Ginger and Pickles cater to the needs of a large assortment of dolls, rabbits, mice, and other diminutive customers. The merchandise on hand includes handkerchiefs, sugar, snuff, and galoshes. In order to keep from frightening their clientele, Ginger and Pickles carefully divide their responsibilities, with Ginger waiting on all the rabbits and Pickles taking care of the mice.

**GIPSY, fictional character; salt and pepper kitchen; created by American writer Booth Tarkington (1869-1946); first appeared in *Penrod and Sam;* housecat who abandons the comforts of civilization for a life among alley cats.**

His extraordinary size, his daring, and his utter lack of sympathy soon made him the leader—and, at the same time, the terror—of all the loose-lived cats in a wide neighborhood. He contracted no friendships and had no confidants. He seldom slept in the same place twice in succession, and though he was wanted by the police, he was not found. In appearance he did not lack distinction of an ominous sort; the slow, rhythmic, perfectly controlled mechanism of his tail, as he impressively

GIPSY

walked abroad, was incomparably sinister. This stately and dangerous walk of his, his long, vibrant whiskers, his scars, his yellow eye, so ice-cold, so fire-hot, haughty as the eye of Satan, gave him the deadly air of a mousequetaire duelist. His soul was in that walk and in that eye; it could be read—the soul of a bravo of fortune, living on his wits and his valour, asking no favours and granting no quarter. Intolerant, proud, sullen, yet watchful and constantly planning—purely a militarist, believing in slaughter as in religion, and confident that art, science, poetry, and the good of the world were happily advanced thereby—Gipsy had become, though technically not a wild cat, undoubtedly the most untamed cat at large in the civilized world.

> Booth Tarkington
> *Penrod and Sam*

**GOREY'S CATS, a selection of illustrated cartoonlike cats created by artist Edward Gorey, which appear in numerous books, including *Catagorey, Amphigorey,* and *Dancing Cats and Neglected Murderesses.***

EDWARD GOREY AND FRIEND
*Photograph by Carl Fisher.*

A GOREY CAT

**H**

**HAMLET, hotel mascot and professional mouser; white with striped tail and gray markings; home, Algonquin Hotel, 59 West 44th Street, New York, NY 10036; subject of book _Algonquin Cat_ (New York, 1980).**

HAMLET
_Photograph by Bill Hayward._

New Yorkers have long been familiar with Hamlet, the personable though sometimes cantankerous cat-in-residence at one of the city's landmark hotels. Hamlet is the current successor to Rusty, who presided over the hotel when its famous literary and theatrical "Round Table" was in session in the 1930s and 1940s. Rusty was so revered that he was given his very own door to the kitchen with his name inscribed above it. This door now belongs to Hamlet.

Hamlet found the Algonquin surpassingly mnrhnh. Cats speak a subtle language in which few sounds carry many meanings, depending on how they are sung and purred. Mnrhnh means comfortable soft chairs. It means fish. It also means fish. It means genial companionship and hello. It means dark aged wood, admiration, permanence, and the absence of dogs. It means fertile for dreams. It was no accident that the Algonquin was also favored by writers, actors, filmmakers, and various other kinds of artists, as well as editors and critics, who gathered there for cocktails like kittens around a bowl of cream. And as a permanent resident, Hamlet himself became a well-known literary figure.

> Val Schaffner
> _Algonquin Cat_

**HARDY'S CAT, pet and literary character; belonged to English writer Thomas Hardy (1840–1928); immortalized in poem "Last Words to a Dumb Friend" (1904).**

Pet was never mourned as you,
Purrer of the spotless hue,
Plumy tail, and wistful gaze
While you humoured our queer ways,
Or outshrilled your morning call
Up the stairs and through the hall—
Foot suspended in its fall—
While, expectant, you would stand
Arched, to meet the stroking hand;
Till your way you chose to wend
Yonder, to your tragic end.

From the chair whereon he sat
Sweep his fur, nor wince thereat;
Rake his little pathways out
Mid the bushes roundabout;
Smooth away his talons' mark
From the claw-worn pine-tree bark,
Where he climbed as dusk embrowned,
Waiting us who loitered round.

Strange it is this speechless thing,
Subject to our mastering,
Subject for his life and food
To our gift, and time, and mood
Timid pensioner of us Powers,
His existence ruled by ours,
Should—by crossing at a breath
Into safe and shielded death,
By the merely taking hence
Of his insignificance—
Loom as largened to the sense,
Shape as part, above man's will,
Of the Imperturbable.
> Thomas Hardy
> "Last Words to a Dumb Friend"

HEATHCLIFF
*The first Heathcliff cartoon, September 3, 1973.*

HEATHCLIFF'S POP

**HEATHCLIFF, comic-strip and animated-cartoon character; created in 1973 by George Gately (1929-  ); named after central figure in Emily Bronte's novel *Wuthering Heights*; appears in seven hundred newspapers and an animated-cartoon show (ABC); subject of book, *Heathcliff Banquet* (New York, 1981).**

Before him, cats were depicted as either stupid or sinister. But cats are smart. Heathcliff represents the anti-hero, like Humphrey Bogart. He's a tough little mug.

People didn't think a cat could carry a comic, but I disagreed. Now there are a lot of other strips, but I don't mind. It's a compliment. There's room for everybody. You just have to stay good.
> George Gately
> Interview in *People* Magazine

*A vanilla fudge sundae and a raw fish!*

## HEMINGWAY'S CATS, several dozen feline pets owned by American writer Ernest Hemingway (1898-1961).

The white tower had been built by Mary in an effort to get the [Hemingways'] complement of thirty cats out of the house, and to provide Ernest with a place more becoming to work in than his bedroom. It worked with the cats but not with Ernest. The ground floor of the tower was the cats' quarters, with special sleeping, eating and maternity accommodations, and they all lived there with the exception of a few favorites like Crazy Christian, Friendless' Brother and Ecstasy, who were allowed house privileges.

A.E. Hotchner
*Papa Hemingway*

## HINSE, pet; belonged to Edinburgh poet Sir Walter Scott (1771-1832).

Ah! cats are a mysterious kind of folk. There is more passing in their minds than we are aware of. It comes no doubt from their being too familiar with warlocks and witches.

Sir Walter Scott

## HODGE, pet; belonged to Samuel Johnson (1709-84), English essayist, biographer, lexicographer, and poet; described by James Boswell (1746-95) in his *Life of Samuel Johnson* (first published, 1791).

I never shall forget the indulgence with which he treated Hodge, his cat; for whom he himself used to go out and buy oysters, lest the servants having that trouble should take a dislike to the poor creature. I am, unluckily, one of those who have an antipathy to a cat, so that I am uneasy when in the room with one; and I own, I frequently suffered a good deal from the presence of the same Hodge. I recollect him one day scrambling up Dr. Johnson's breast, apparently with much satisfaction, while my friend, smiling and half-whistling, rubbed down his back, and pulled him by the tail; and when I observed he was a fine cat, saying, "Why, yes, Sir, but I have had cats whom I liked better than this;" and then, as if perceiving Hodge to be out of countenance, adding, "but he is a very fine cat, a very fine cat indeed."

James Boswell
*The Life of Samuel Johnson*

ERNEST HEMINGWAY
*The author and one of his forty cats, Cuba, 1952.*
*Photograph by Peter Buckley.*

HODGE

**JAKE**, fictional character; also known as "The Cat From Outer Space"; starred in movie of the same name with humans Ken Berry, Sandy Duncan, and McLean Stevenson (Walt Disney Productions, 1978); Jake, portrayed by a Hollywood feline named Rumple, arrived on earth in a spaceship he controlled with his mind, and used his magic collar to keep hapless earthlings out of trouble.

**JENNIE**, fictional character; stray tabby; created by Paul Gallico (1897-1976); first appeared in *The Abandoned* (New York, 1950); protector of Peter, a little boy turned into a white cat and set loose in London.

JENNIE

"When in doubt—any kind of doubt—*Wash!* That is Rule No. 1," said Jennie. She sat now primly and a little stiffly, with her tail wrapped around her feet, near the head of the big bed beneath the Napoleon Initial and Crown, rather like a schoolmistress. But it was obvious that the role of teacher and the respectful attention Peter bestowed upon her were not unendurable, because she had a pleased expression and her eyes were again gleaming brightly.

The sun had reached its noon zenith in the sky in the world that lay outside the dark and grimy warehouse, and coming in slantwise through the small window sent a dusty shaft that fell like a theatrical spotlight about Jennie's head and shoulders as she lectured.

"If you have committed any kind of an error and anyone scolds you —wash," she was saying. "If you slip and fall off something and somebody laughs at you—wash. If you are getting the worst of an argument and want to break off hostilities until you have composed yourself, start washing. Remember, *every* cat respects another cat at her toilet. That's our first rule of social deportment, and you must also observe it."

Paul Gallico
*The Abandoned*

**JEOFFRY**, pet cat and literary character; belonged to poet Christopher Smart (1722-1771); described in poem "Jubilate Agno" ("Rejoice in the Lamb," 1759-

**63); Smart's only companion during his four-year confinement in a London madhouse.**

For I will consider my Cat Jeoffry.

For he is the servant of the Living God duly and daily serving him.

For at the first glance of the glory of God in the East he worships in his way.

For is this done by wreathing his body seven times round with elegant quickness.

For then he leaps up to catch the musk, which is the blessing of God upon his prayer.

For he rolls upon prank to work it in.

For having done duty and received blessing he begins to consider himself.

For this he performs in ten degrees.

For first he looks upon his fore-paws to see if they are clean.

For secondly he kicks up behind to clear away there.

For thirdly he works it upon stretch with the fore-paws extended.

For fourthly he sharpens his paws by wood.

For fifthly he washes himself.

For Sixthly he rolls upon wash.

For Seventhly he fleas himself, that he may not be interrupted upon the beat.

For Eighthly he rubs himself against a post.

For Ninthly he looks up for his instructions.

For Tenthly he goes in quest of food.

For having consider'd God and himself he will consider his neighbor.

For if he meets another cat he will kiss her in kindness.

For when he takes his prey he plays with it to give it a chance.

For one mouse in seven escapes by his dallying.

For when his day's work is done his business more properly begins.

For he keeps the Lord's watch in the night against the adversary.

For he counteracts the powers of darkness by his electrical skin & glaring eyes.

For he counteracts the Devil, who is death, by brisking about the life.

For in his morning orisons he loves the sun and the sun loves him.

For he is of the tribe of Tiger.

Christopher Smart<br>"Jubilate Agno"

JEOFFRY
*"…he washes himself.…" Drawing by Watteau.*

**JONES,** orange-striped cat featured in the movie *Alien,* (20th Century-Fox, 1979, one of two survivors of the attack on the ship *Nostromo*.

**JOSEPH,** pet and millionaire; striped tom; belonged to Agatha Isabel Frazer Higgins; home, England; weight forty-eight pounds; became wealthy in 1969 when Miss Higgins died and left him her fortune.

**KAROUN,** pet; also known as "the king of cats"; belonged to French writer Jean Cocteau (1889–1963); dedicatee of Cocteau's *Drole de Menage*.

# K

JONES
*And co-star Sigourney Weaver in "Alien."*

KAROUN
*Drawing by Jean Cocteau.*

DRÔLE DE MÉNAGE

I love cats because I love my home, and little by little they become its visible soul. A kind of active silence emanates from these furry beasts who appear deaf to orders, to appeals, to reproaches and who move in a

completely royal authority through the network of our acts, retaining only those which intrigue them or comfort them.

Jean Cocteau

**KLIBAN'S CATS, cartoon characters; nameless; created by B. (Bernard) Kliban (1935- ); first appeared in *Cat* (New York, 1975); favorite foods include cheese sandwiches, ham, mice.**

Kliban's cats are an odd assortment of striped and sometimes sneakered felines who were an instant hit when they were first introduced to the public in 1975. Generally defined as "One Hell of a nice animal, frequently mistaken for a meatloaf," Kliban's cats are now the center of a $50-million spin-off empire, including calendars, umbrellas, housewares, dolls, purses, ice buckets, greeting cards, stationery, bed sheets, wrapping paper, and dozens of other items. Such mind-boggling success proves that cat lovers aren't the sentimental fools that dog worshippers, among others, sometimes make them out to be: Kliban's humor is razor edged, and his drawings sometimes border on the grotesque. "Man lying to a cat," for example, is no ordinary title for a kitty cartoon. Nor is the following an ordinary theme song: "Love to eat them mousies/Mousies what I love to eat/Bite they little heads off/Nibble on they tiny feet."

Kliban fans shouldn't hold their breaths for *Cat II,* unfortunately. The artist is uncomfortable with his success and with the blizzard of fan mail it has produced. (Crazy little old ladies, he claims, are always writing to ask him how to care for their pets.) Kliban's more recent collections have been conspicuously empty of cats. "Cats are wonderful," Kliban once said. "It's drawings of cats I get tired of."

There were a total of four cats [in my life]. Twelve years ago, my wife bought the first one, Noko Marie, for three dollars. We kept one male, Norton, from the first litter. And we kept Nitty from the second batch. Nitty was my favorite—a big, fat, striped cat. Then some little kids gave my wife a stray we named Burton Rustle. As a kid, I used to hate them because I was violently allergic, but I loved those four cats. One day Norton just disappeared. It almost broke my heart. Nitty got feline leukemia and died in my arms—that did break my heart. I haven't seen the other two in a long time. I hope they're okay. I get very sentimental about pets. That's why I don't want another one. When they died, it nearly did me in.

B. Kliban
Interviewed in *Rolling Stone,* 1978

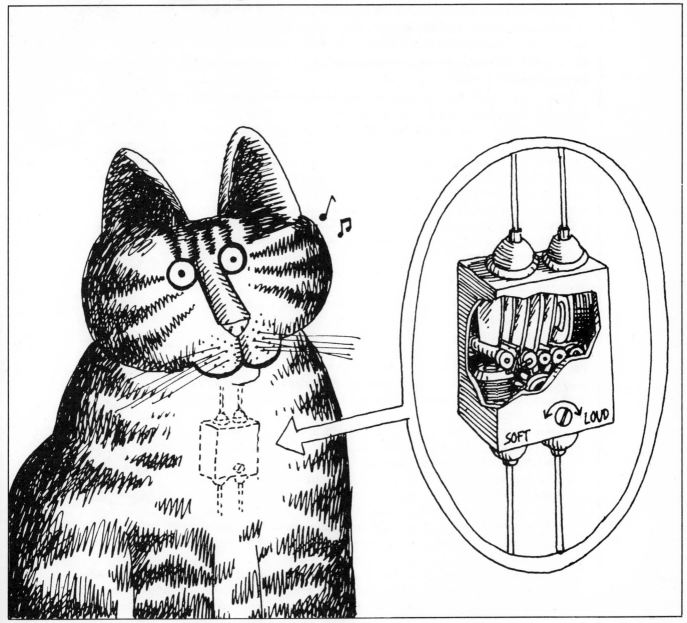

**KRAZY KAT, comic-strip character; created by George Herriman (1880-1944); home, Coconino County; role in life: to be loved and to be hit on the head with a brick by Ignatz Mouse; characteristic saying: "I'm a heppy, heppy 'ket'!"**

HERRIMAN

*Krazy Kat* is widely held by comic enthusiasts to be the greatest comic strip of all time, which, of course, makes Krazy Kat the greatest comic-strip *cat* of all time. Felix and Garfield fans may disagree, but almost from the very beginning, Krazy Kat earned the admiration of the leading thinkers and artists of his day. Although the strip was never a huge commercial success, Krazy inspired fierce loyalties in millions of faithful followers and earned a sort of honorary position in contemporary literature. Herriman was treated more as a literary genius than as a comic-strip artist, and Krazy Kat became an intellectual folk hero. President Woodrow Wilson, among many others, was an unflagging fan. Dramatist John Alden Carpenter made Krazy the subject of an entire ballet in 1922. Two years later, critic Gilbert Seldes wrote an extremely favorable essay about Krazy in a book called *The Seven Lively Arts.*

KRAZY KAT

Krazy made his (or *her,* according to some authorities; Herriman changed his mind from time to time) first comic appearance as a minor character in the June 20, 1910 edition of Herriman's *Dingbat Family* strip in the now-defunct New York *Journal.* He was first referred to as "Krazy Kat" a month later in the August 17 strip. On October 28, 1918, the entire strip took his name, and in 1916 a full-page color Sunday strip was added. That same year, Krazy appeared in a number of animated cartoons produced by Hearst-Vitaphone. Through it all, Krazy had the company of a large and sometimes wild group of friends, including Ignatz Mouse, Offissa Pupp, Joe Stork, Kolin Kelly, Sancho Pansy, Don Kiyote, Mr. Meeyowl, Mrs. Kwakk-wakk, and many others.

OFFISSA PUPP AND IGNATZ

Krazy's strip was always something special. Herriman liked to play with comic-strip conventions and was always toying with the reader's perception of reality. The backgrounds of his comic scenes changed, sometimes wildly, from one panel to the next, and Krazy was once spied on by characters in the Herriman strip above his on the page. Krazy made his last appearance in 1944, the year of Herriman's death.

*right:*
KRAZY KAT AND
THE TELEPHONE
*A failure to communicate.*

[Krazy Kat] is a living ideal. She is a spiritual force, inhabiting a merely real world—and the realer a merely real world happens to be, the more this living ideal becomes herself. Hence—needless to add—

CONT'D →

the brick. Only if, and whenever, that kind of reality (cruelly wielded by our heroic villain, Ignatz Mouse, in despite of our villainous hero, Offissa Pupp) smites Krazy—fairly and squarely—does the joyous symbol of Love Fulfilled appear above our triumphantly unknowledgeable heroine. And now do we understand the meaning of democracy? If we don't, a poet-painter called George Herriman most certainly cannot be blamed. Democracy, he tells us again and again, isn't some ultraprogressive myth of a superbenevolent World As Should Be. The meteoric burlesk melodrama of a democracy is a struggle between society (Offissa Pupp) and the individual (Ignatz Mouse) over an ideal (our heroine)—a struggle from which, again and again and again, emerges one stupendous fact: namely, that the ideal of democracy fulfills herself only if, and whenever, society fails to suppress the individual.

e.e. cummings

# M

**MATTERHORN CAT, adventurer and pet; belonged to Josephine Aufdenblatten of Geneva, Switzerland; climbed the Matterhorn unassisted at age of four months.**

The kitten, accustomed to watch from the hotel home the dawn departure of climbers, decided one morning to follow in their footsteps. He was soon left behind, but after a long and lonely climb reached the Solway hut (12,556 ft.). The next day he climbed still higher, and when night fell bivouacked in a *couloir* above the shoulder.

The next morning he was seen by a group of climbers, who passed him by, convinced that his climbing skill, if not his spirit, would be defeated by the difficult Ropes, Slabs and the Roof. They were wrong, and hours later the cat, miauing and tail up, reached the summit (14,780 ft.), where the incredulous climbing party rewarded him with a share in their meal.

*The Times* of London
September 7, 1950

**MEHITABEL, literary character; created by American writer Don Marquis (1878-1937); first appeared in *archy and mehitabel* (New York, 1927).**

Mehitabel is an alley cat whose life and opinions have been described by an industrious typing cockroach named Archy. Archy types by the hunt-and-jump method and is therefore unable to use any of the upper-case characters on the typewriter of his "boss," the human poet usually given credit for Archy's productions. This is why there are no capital letters or punctuation marks (except where Archy has gone to the trouble of spelling them out) in the sample reproduced below.

Mehitabel, according to Archy, claims to have a human soul; indeed, she believes she was Cleopatra in a previous life and that she is now an alley cat owing to a "transmigration of souls." Archy is at least a little skeptical of Mehitabel's claims, but he transcribes them faithfully and comments with some sadness on the low state to which she seems to have fallen. He is also forgiving of Mehitabel, pointing out that her glorious past "was a long time ago/and one must not be/surprised if mehitabel/has forgotten some of her/more regal habits." Mehitabel herself is stoical about her circumstances, dismissing any hint of mournfulness with the exclamation "wotthehell wotthehell."

mehitabel the cat claims that
she has a human soul
also and has transmigrated
from body to body and it
may be so boss you
remember i told you she accused
herself of being cleopatra once i
asked her about antony

antony who she asked me are
you thinking of that
song about rowley and gammon and
spinach heigho for antony rowley

no i said mark antony the
great roman the friend of
caesar surely cleopatra you
remember j caesar

listen archy she said i
have been so many different
people in my time and met
so many prominent gentlemen i
wont lie to you or stall i
do get my dates mixed sometimes

I WAS CLEOPATRA ONCE
SHE SAID.

think of how much i have had a
chance to forget and i have
always made a point of not
carrying grudges over
from one life to the next archy

i have been
used something fierce in my time but
i am no bum sport archy
i am a free spirit archy i
look on myself as being
quite a romantic character oh the
queens i have been and the
swell feeds i have ate
a cockroach which you are

and a poet which you used to be
archy couldn t understand
my feelings at having come
down to this i have
had bids to elegant feeds where poets
and cockroaches would
neither one be mentioned without a
laugh archy i have had
adventures but i
have never been an adventuress
one life up and the next life
down archy but always a lady
through it all and a
good mixer too always the
life of the party archy but never
anything vulgar always free footed
archy never tied down to
a job or housework yes looking
back on it all i can say is
i had some romantic
lives and some elegant times i
have seen better days archy but
what is the use of kicking kid its
all in the game like a gentleman

friend of mine used to say
toujours gai kid toujours gai he
was an elegant cat he used
to be a poet himself and he made up
some elegant poetry about me and him

> Don Marquis
> "mehitabel s extensive past"

**MICETTO, pet; gray red with black stripes; belonged to Pope Leo XII (1760-1829); given to Vicomte Francois Rene de Chateaubriand (1768-1848), French ambassador to Rome, when Leo realized he was dying.**

MICETTO

**MIN, pet and literary character; belonged to American writer Henry David Thoreau (1817-1862).**

Min caught a mouse, and was playing with it in the yard. It had got away from her once or twice and she had caught it again, and now it was stealing off again, as she was complacently watching it with her paws tucked under her, when her friend, Riorden, a stout cock, stepped up inquisitively, looked down at the mouse with one eye, turning its head, then picked it up by the tail, gave it two or three whacks on the ground, and giving it a dexterous toss in the air, caught the mouse in its open mouth. It went, head foremost and alive, down Riorden's capacious throat in the twinkling of an eye, never again to be seen in this world; Min all the while, with paws comfortably tucked under her, looked on unconcerned. What did one mouse matter, more or less, to her? The cock walked off amid the currant-bushes, stretched his neck up and gulped once or twice, and the deed was accomplished. It might be set down among the *Gesta gallorum*. There were several human witnesses. It is a question whether Min ever understood where that mouse went to. She sits composedly sentinel, with paws tucked under her, a good part of her days at present, by some ridiculous little hole, the possible entry of a mouse.

> Henry David Thoreau

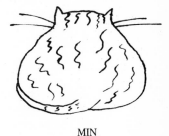

MIN

**MINERVA, fictional character; featured on television program *Our Miss Brooks;* see also ORANGEY.**

**MINNALOUSHE, literary character; black; created by Irish poet William Butler Yeats (1865-1939); first appeared in poem "The Cat and the Moon" (1919).**

MINNALOUSHE

The cat went here and there
And the moon spun round like a top,
And the nearest kin of the moon,
The creeping cat, looked up.
Black Minnaloushe stared at the moon,
For, wander and wail as he would,
The pure cold light in the sky
Troubled his animal blood.
Minnaloushe runs in the grass
Lifting his delicate feet.
Do you dance, Minnaloushe, do you dance?
When two close kindred meet,
What better than call a dance?
Maybe the moon may learn,
Tired of that courtly fashion,
A new dance turn.
Minnaloushe creeps through the grass
From moonlit place to place,
The sacred moon overhead
Has taken a new phase.
Does Minnaloushe know that his pupils
Will pass from change to change,
And that from round to crescent,
From crescent to round they range?
Minnaloushe creeps through the grass
Alone, important and wise,
And lifts to the changing moon
His changing eyes.

William Butler Yeats
"The Cat and the Moon"

**MISTY MALARKY YING YANG, pet; male Siamese; first feline of the Jimmy Carter administration; belongs to President Carter's daughter Amy.**

Misty joined the Carter family during the 1976 campaign and spent all four years of the President's term living in the White House.

*right:*
MISTY MALARKY YING YANG
*Amy Carter's kitty, the most recent of many distinguished cats to have had the run of the White House.*

**MORRIS, television and motion-picture personality; orange tiger; birth date unknown; television debut, "9-Lives Presents Morris," cat-food commercial, 1969; died 1978 of natural causes.**

Morris, the pudgy orange cat who rode to stardom as the finicky salesman of 9-Lives cat food, was almost certainly the most famous stray cat who ever lived. He was discovered in 1968 at the Humane Society of Hinsdale, Illinois, a prosperous suburb of Chicago. When noted animal trainer Bob Martwick visited the shelter on a talent hunt for a mattress manufacturer, Morris was living in a cramped cage on the Human Society's death row. If Martwick hadn't come along when he did, Morris might very well have been put to sleep to make room for more recent arrivals, and the world would never have known its greatest feline star. But Morris and the world were lucky. Martwick spotted his natural talent (the star-to-be stayed where he was put and was almost impossible to distract) and paid five dollars for his release.

ANNCR: (VO) Nine-Lives presents Morris.

Later in the year, Morris beat out an enormous field of furry hopefuls to win a place in a planned advertising campaign for 9-Lives. Morris was so exceptionally poised that the ad campaign was quickly rewritten to feature him as a star. The commercial's producers had never seen anything like him before. He was given his name (up until this point, he had been known as Lucky) and star billing. Later, he was made an honorary director of Star-Kist Foods, Inc., 9-Lives' parent company, and was given the power to veto new cat-food flavors that didn't strike his fancy.

LADY: Din din, Morris.

Morris was such an unprecedented phenomenon that he was given a special Patsy Award (the Oscar of the animal world) for "outstanding performance in a TV commercial" in 1973. He was even chosen to co-star with Dyan Cannon and Burt Reynolds in the popular movie *Shamus*.

Like most celebrities, Morris found that his lifestyle followed his fortunes in the acting world. Once nothing more than a humble stray, he now found himself being invited to appear on countless television shows. He was chauffeured from one appointment to another in sleek black limousines and was even given an elegant—and extremely expensive—Vuitton litter box. He ate at fancy restaurants, sometimes accompanied by fashionable kitties of the opposite sex, and hobnobbed with Hollywood stars. Once he even visited the White House and signed a bill making an ink impression with his paw. No cat has ever gone so far from such humble beginnings or been loved by so many.

LADY: Super Supper? Beef and Liver

MORRIS

*The world's most finicky cat in one of the commercials that made him famous.*

LADY: I found this in the attic!
MORRIS: It's not my side of the family.

LADY: Where should I hang it?

MORRIS: In the garage!

MORRIS: I'll eat when the moose eats!

LADY: Don't be finicky. There's Nine-Lives.

MORRIS: Maybe I'll start without him.

MORRIS: Nine-Lives Beef and Liver! Yum yum!

ANNCR: (VO) Nine-Lives, nutritious foods cats really like.

Even Morris. MORRIS: They can stuff me with Nine-Lives anytime. (SFX: LIP SMACK)

**MORRIS II, television personality; orange tiger; birth date unknown; current home, Chicago, Illinois.**

When Morris died in 1978, the people at 9-Lives began combing through hundreds of photographs and mailing out urgent bulletins to humane societies all over the country, hoping to find a cat with enough star quality to take the master's place. The search took two and a half years. It finally ended in a nondescript humane society on the East Coast with a youthful orange tiger who looked so much like the original Morris that all but the most devoted fans have trouble telling them apart. Most important of all, the new kitty shared Morris' superfeline ability for staying where he was put and patiently enduring barrages of flash bulbs and torrents of applause. The star now lives with Morris's old owner and trainer, Bob Martwick, and makes regular appearances in the cat-food commercials that have become classics of American popular culture.

I've always allowed cats a certain kind of unique quality, but I certainly never thought of them as being stars of any sort. You know, they're just animals, for God's sake. So are people, for that matter, but even so I've never had much truck with famous individuals just for the sake of their fame, unless they've got some special talent. And this cat seemed just to *sit* there. But then, at our first book signing, at a B. Dalton, I looked at all the people who had stood in line on a rainy day to meet this cat, and I saw how their eyes lit up when they saw him, and I realized that this cat was really *special*. There's something quite meaningful about him. Thirty-nine out of forty people on the street recognize him, and that, I think, is really amazing.

Barbara Burn<br>Morris II's biographer

MORRIS II
*A star is reborn.*

## MOTHER GOOSE'S CATS, literary figures.

Felines figure importantly in the large collection of nursery rhymes familiar to English-speaking children as the works of Mother Goose. Of uncertain origin, Mother Goose's rhymes date from at least the 17th Century.

Ding dong bell,
Pussy's in the well.
Who put her in?
Little Johnny Green.
Who pulled her out?
Little Tommy Stout.

What a naughty boy was that,
To drown a poor Pussy Cat,
Who never did any Harm,
And killed the mice in his father's barn.

High diddle, diddle,
The Cat and the fiddle,
   The cow jumped over the moon.
The little dog laughed
To see such sport
   And the dish ran away with the spoon.

Pussy Cat, Pussy Cat, where have you been?
   I've been to London to look at the queen.
Pussy Cat, Pussy Cat, what did you there?
   I frightened a little mouse under her chair.

Six little mice sat down to spin;
Pussy passed by and she peeped in.
What are you doing, my little men?
Weaving coats for gentlemen.
Shall I come in and cut off your threads?
No, no, Mistress Pussy, you'd bite off our heads.
Oh, no, I'll not; I'll help you to spin.
That may be so, but you can't come in.
Says Puss: You look so wondrous wise,
I like your whiskers and bright black eyes;
Your house is the nicest house I see;
I think there is room for you and for me.
The mice were so pleased that they opened the door,
And Pussy soon had them all dead on the floor.

I love little Pussy,
   Her coat is so warm,
And if I don't hurt her,
   She'll do me no harm.

So I'll not pull her tail,
   Nor drive her away,
But Pussy and I
   Very gently will play.

She shall sit by my side,
   And I'll give her some food;
And Pussy will love me
   Because I am good.

**MOUSCHI, pet; belonged to Anne Frank (1929–1945); described in *Diary of a Young Girl* (first published, 1947); one of two cats living with the Franks, Van Daans, and others in their secret hideout from the Nazis.**

We were sitting in the attic doing some French yesterday afternoon when I suddenly heard water pattering down behind me. I asked Peter what it could be, but he didn't even reply, simply tore up to the loft, where the source of the disaster was, and pushed Mouschi, who, because of the wet earth box, had sat down beside it, harshly back to the right place. A great din and disturbance followed, and Mouschi, who had finished by that time, dashed downstairs.

Mouschi, seeking the convenience of something similar to his box, had chosen some wood shavings. The pool had trickled down from the loft into the attic immediately and, unfortunately, landed just beside and in the barrel of potatoes. The ceiling was dripping, and as the attic floor is not free from holes either, several yellow drips came through the ceiling into the dining room between a pile of stockings and some books, which were lying on the table. I was doubled up with laughter, it really was a scream. There was Mouschi crouching under a chair, Peter with water, bleaching powder, and floor cloth, and Van Daan trying to soothe everyone. The calamity was soon over, but it's a well-known fact that cats' puddles positively stink. The potatoes proved this only too clearly and also the wood shavings, that Daddy had collected in a bucket to be burned. Poor Mouschi! How were you to know that peat is unobtainable?

> Anne Frank
> *Diary of a Young Girl*

**MTM KITTEN, corporate mascot; name unknown; appears in logo of MTM (Mary Tyler Moore) Enterprises, Inc., television production company; first used, 1970.**

When the people at MTM decided to make their mascot a kitten, in parodied tribute to the famous roaring-lion logo of the old Metro-Goldwyn-Mayer film studios, they turned not to a professional cat from a Hollywood talent agency, but to a litter of strictly amateur kittens belonging to the son of one of the company's film editors. An MTM camera crew staked out the kittens for most of a day, hoping to capture a toothy head-on meow, but the kittens simply wouldn't cooperate. The crew was ready to scrap the project until the editor realized he could produce an acceptable roar by reversing a piece of film in which one of the kittens yawned. The rest is history.

MTM KITTEN
*The yawn that became a roar.*

NEMO

*England's Prime Feline, with Harold Wilson and family.*

**MUEZZA, legendary figure; favorite cat of Mohammed.**

Mohammed was so fond of cats, according to legend, that he once cut off his sleeve rather than disturb his beloved Muezza, who was sleeping in his arms.

# N

**NEMO, pet; Siamese; belonged to former British Prime Minister Harold Wilson (1916-   ); home, #10 Downing Street, London.**

**NITCHEVO, fictional character; created by Tennessee Williams (1914-  ); first appeared in story "The Malediction" (1948).**

You could see that Nitchevo did not take stock in chance. She believed that everything progressed according to a natural, predestined order and that there was nothing to be apprehensive about. All of her movements were slow and without agitation. They were accomplished with a consummate grace. Her amber eyes regarded each object with unblinking serenity. Even about her food she made no haste. Each evening Lucio brought home a pint of milk for her supper and breakfast: Nitchevo sat quietly waiting on her haunches while he poured it into the cracked saucer borrowed from the landlady and set it on the floor beside the bed. Then he lay down on the bed, expectantly watching, while Nitchevo came slowly forward to the pale blue saucer. She looked up at him once—slowly—with her unflickering yellow eyes before she started to eat, and then she gracefully lowered her small chin to the saucer's edge, the red satin tip of tongue protruded and the room was filled with the sweet, faint music of her gently lapping.

                    Tennessee Williams
                    "The Malediction"

NITCHEVO

# O

**OLLIE, British comic-strip character; orange alley cat with enormous feet; created by Harry Hargreaves (1922-   ); also known as "Ollie the Merry Mouser"; first appeared in "Ollie the Alley Cat" strip (1951).**

**ORANGEY, motion-picture and television personality; orange tiger; cinematic debut, title role in *Rhubarb* (1952); won Patsy Awards 1952, 1962; also appeared in *Gigot, Breakfast at Tiffany's,* and in TV series *Our Miss Brooks;* died 1963 of natural causes.**

Orangey could have been Morris's twin. Both cats are photogenic tigers with thick, luxuriant orange fur. They had the same satisfied, well-fed faces and the same fluffy, raccoonlike tails. They even weighed the same, about fourteen pounds. The most loyal Morris fan might have trouble telling the two cats apart by looking at their photographs.

Actually, the similarities between Orangey and Morris did not extend very far beneath the fur. Where Morris was placid and imperturbable, with a cool stage sense that enabled him to remain perfectly still on camera even if he was being doused with water, Orangey was a cantankerous prima donna who was disliked even by his trainer and who once required twenty-two doubles for filming a difficult scene. A movie executive called him "the world's meanest cat." During one shooting session, Orangey's trainer, Frank Inn, had to place guard dogs at all the doors of the movie studio in order to dissuade the star from running away—something he had done the day before. But the trouble was worth it, and Orangey won more awards than any other cat in show business before or since.

> My cat is an actor, the best in the world, and can play any part.
>> Frank Inn
>> Owner and trainer

**OSCAR, pet and literary character; belonged to writer H.P. Lovecraft; killed by an automobile; immortalized in eight-line epitaph by Lovecraft.**

> Damn'd be this harsh mechanick age
>> That whirls us fast and faster,
> And swallows with Sabazian rage
>> Nine lives in one disaster.
>
> I take my quill with sadden'd thought,
>> Tho' falt'ringly I do it;
> And having curst the Juggernaut,
>> Inscribe: OSCARVS FUIT!
>>> H.P. Lovecraft
>>> "Elegy to Oscar, a Dead Cat"

# P

**PEPPER, motion-picture personality; gray; birth date unknown; home, Hollywood.**

Very few cats have attained genuine star status in films over the years since most of the really big roles are written for dogs or horses. But despite this apparent prejudice against felines, a handful of cats have managed to become Hollywood legends. The very first of these was Pepper, a quick-witted alley cat who worked alongside such motion-picture greats as Charlie Chaplin, Fatty Arbuckle, and the Keystone Kops in Mack Sennett's legendary stable of comic stars.

Pepper came into the movies not through the back door but through the floor. The friendly kitten climbed out from under a broken plank on a shooting set at Sennett's famous stuido one day and was so captivating that the director on the set scooped her up and immediately worked her into the scene he was shooting. The cat performed flawlessly, and when the scene was completed, Sennett told her, "From henceforth you shall be known as Pepper, and I predict a long and brilliant career for another member of the Sennett realm." The Hollywood titan later said that Pepper was "as disarming as the lovely Lillian Gish."

One of Pepper's most celebrated co-stars was a kindhearted Great Dane named Teddy, who worked with his favorite leading kitten in a number of Sennett movies. So great was Pepper's attachment to Teddy that when the dog died, Pepper refused to work. She stopped cooperating with directors and turned up her nose at the numerous dogs who were tried out as Teddy's replacement. After several days of mourning, she simply disappeared from the set and was never seen again.

> She had courage, that kitty. A lesson for all of us if a time like hers ever comes into our lives. She retired at the top. That's where her name will always shine. And I don't want no trainers hawking any other pussy around here! Pepper's our first and our last feline star!
> Mack Sennett

**PRACTICAL CATS, fictional characters; described in *Old Possum's Book of Practical Cats* (1939) by T.S. Eliot (1888–1965); individual cats mentioned include Macavity, Mr. Mistoffelees, Gus, Bustopher Jones, Jennyanydots, Growltiger, Mungojerrie, Rumpelteazer, Shimbleshanks, and the Rum Tum Tugger.**

The Rum Tum Tugger is a Curious Cat:
If you offer him pheasant he would rather have grouse.
If you put him in a house he would much prefer a flat,
If you put him in a flat then he'd rather have a house.
If you set him on a mouse then he only wants a rat,
If you set him on a rat then he'd rather chase a mouse.
Yes the Rum Tum Tugger is a Curious Cat—
   And there isn't any call for me to shout it:
     For he will do
     As he do do
       And there's no doing anything about it!

The Rum Tug Tugger is a terrible bore:
When you let him in, then he wants to be out;
He's always on the wrong side of the door,
And as soon as he's at home, then he'd like to get about.
He likes to lie in the bureau drawer,
But he makes such a fuss if he can't get out.
Yes the Rum Tum Tugger is a Curious Cat—
   And it isn't any use for you to doubt it:
     For he will do
     As he do do
       And there's no doing anything about it!

The Rum Tum Tugger is a curious beast:
His disobliging ways are a matter of habit.
If you offer him fish then he always wants a feast;
When there isn't any fish then he won't eat rabbit.
If you offer him cream then he sniffs and sneers,
For he only likes what he finds for himself;
So you'll catch him in it right up to the ears,
If you put it away on the larder shelf.
The Rum Tum Tugger is artful and knowing,
The Rum Tum Tugger doesn't care for a cuddle;
But he'll leap on your lap in the middle of your sewing,
For there's nothing he enjoys like a horrible muddle.
Yes the Rum Tum Tugger is a Curious Cat—
   And there isn't any need for me to spout it:
     For he will do

PRACTICAL CAT
*Drawing by Steinlen.*

As he do do
   And there's no doing anything about it!
      T.S. Eliot
      "The Rum Tum Tugger"

**PRUDENCE, pet; blue Persian; belonged to former French President Georges Clemenceau (1841-1929).**

**PUFF, fictional character; featured in dozens of children's books published by Scott, Foresman since 1917; played with Dick, Jane, and Sally and was chased by Spot, the dog.**

PUFF
*Having a ball.*

Jane said, "See the pets.
See the pets come to the house.

"Run to the house, Sally," said Dick.
"Come with the pets.
"Come with Spot and Puff.
Run, run! Run to the house.
Run to the house with the pets."
      from *We Look and See*

**PUSS, pet and recordholder; tabby; belonged to Mrs. T. Holloway of England; oldest cat on record; died November 28, 1939, aged thirty-six years and one day.**

**PUSS IN BOOTS, fictional character; also known as the "Master Cat"; origins unknown; immortalized by Charles Perrault, French writer, (1628-1703), in *Contes du temps passe* (1697).**

Puss is a classic figure from a classic fairy tale. He uses his ingenuity and cunning to raise his lowly master to a position of great power, and in doing so he elevates himself as well. Any cat owner who secretly suspects that his pet harbors greater mental powers than cats are usually given credit for will find it impossible not to be delighted by the story.

As Perrault's tale begins, we meet a young man whose father, a modest miller, has just died. The miller's worldly goods at the time of his death amount to nothing more than his mill, his ass, and his cat. Because the young man has two elder brothers, he is forced to accept the cat as his entire inheritance, and he immediately despairs of his future. His only recourse, he says, will be to eat the cat and make a muff out of its fur.

When the cat, whose name is Puss, overhears what the young man plans to do with him, he immediately realizes that he will have to think of something fast if he wishes to save his skin. Hitting on a plan, he tells his new owner that there is no need for him to worry.

"All you have to do," Puss says, "is to give me a pouch, and get a pair of boots made for me so that I can walk in the woods."

The young man is skeptical, but because his situation seems so desperate, he decides he has nothing to lose by following the cat's instructions. He gives Puss the items he has requested and leaves the rest to fate.

Puss slips on his boots and uses his pouch to snare a young rabbit, which he then presents to the king, saying it is a gift from "the marquis of Carabas." The king is very pleased and does not know that the marquis of Carabas is merely the high-sounding name that Puss has given to his master.

Over the next few months, Puss makes more gifts to the king, always in the name of "the marquis of Carabas," a figure who begins to grow in the king's imagination. At last Puss uses his cunning to arrange a meeting between his master and the king's daughter, a beautiful young princess who is the pride of the entire kingdom.

The young man and the princess fall in love at first sight, and the

king, still believing that he is in the presence of a great nobleman, immediately offers her hand in marriage. The princess and the "marquis" live happily ever after, and Puss, by now a figure of great repute, retires from the business of hunting mice.

**PUSSY-CAT, fictional character; created by English artist, writer, and humorist Edward Lear (1812–88); first appeared in "The Owl and the Pussy-cat"; see also FOSS.**

The Owl and the Pussy-cat went to sea
   In a beautiful pea-green boat:
They took some honey, and plenty of money
   Wrapped up in a five-pound note.
The Owl looked up to the stars above,
   And sang to a small guitar,
"O lovely Pussy, O Pussy, my love,
  What a beautiful Pussy you are,
      You are,
      You are!
  What a beautiful Pussy you are!"

THE OWL AND THE PUSSY-CAT
*Drawing by Edward Lear.*

Pussy said to the Owl, "You elegant fowl,
  How charmingly sweet you sing!
Oh! let us be married; too long we have tarried;
  But what shall we do for a ring?"
They sailed away, for a year and a day,
  To the land where the bong-tree grows;
And there in a wood a Piggy-wig stood,
  With a ring at the end of his nose,
      His nose,
      His nose,
  With a ring at the end of his nose.

"Dear Pig, are you willing to sell for one shilling
  Your ring?" Said the Piggy, "I will."
So they took it away, and were married next day
  By the Turkey who lives on the hill.
They dined on mince and slices of quince,
  Which they ate with a runcible spoon;
And hand in hand, on the edge of the sand,
  They danced by the light of the moon,
      The moon,
      The moon,
  They danced by the light of the moon.

      Edward Lear
      "The Owl and the Pussy-cat"

**PUSSYCAT PRINCESS, comic-strip character; created by Grace C. Drayton (1877-1936); first appeared March 10, 1935; drawn by Ruth Carroll after Drayton's death.**

Pussycat Princess was an overcute feline with a supporting cast made up entirely of cats. Dialogue in Pussycat's strip was riddled with bad puns, and she never had a very wide following. The strip made its last appearance on July 13, 1947.

**PYEWACKET, movie star cat who won the Patsy Award for his role as a modern-day witch's cat in *Bell, Book and Candle* (1959); co-starred with James Stewart, Kim Novak, Jack Lemmon, and Ernie Kovacs.**

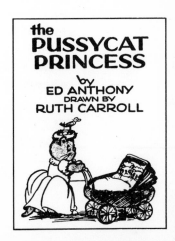

the
PUSSYCAT
PRINCESS
by
ED ANTHONY
DRAWN BY
RUTH CARROLL

# R

**REYNOLDS'S CAT, pet and literary character; belonged to wife of English poet John Hamilton Reynolds (1796-1852); immortalized in sonnet by Reynolds's friend, the poet John Keats (1795-1821).**

> Cat! who hast pass'd thy grand climacteric,
>> How many mice and rats hast in thy days
>> Destroy'd—How many tit bits stolen? Gaze
> With those bright languid segments green, and prick
> Those velvet ears—but pr'ythee do not stick
>> Thy latent talons in me—and unpraise
>> Thy gentle mew—and tell me all the frays
> Of fish and mice, and rats and tender chick.
> Nay, look not down, nor lick thy dainty wrists—
>> For all the wheezy asthma,—and for all
> Thy tail's tip is nick'd off—and though the fists
>> Of many a maid have given thee many a maul,
> Still is that fur as soft as when the lists
>> In youth thou enter'dst on glass bottled wall.
>> > John Keats
>> > "To a Cat"

**RHUBARB, fictional character; created by American writer H. Allen Smith in novel of the same name (New York, 1950); portrayed by cat actor ORANGEY (see separate entry) in 1951 Paramount movie which also starred Ray Milland, Jan Sterling, and Gene Lockhart; in Smith's novel and the subsequent movie, Rhubarb became the owner of the Brooklyn Dodgers after inheriting a fortune from his owner.**

**RICHELIEU'S CATS, pets; belonged to French Cardinal Armand Jean du Plessis, Duc de Richelieu (1585-1642); noted for their number and the devotion of their master.**

With Richelieu the taste for cats was a mania; when he rose in the morning and when he went to bed at night he was always surrounded by a dozen of them with which he played, delighting to watch them

11476-59

jump and gambol. He had one of his chambers fitted up as a cattery, which was entrusted to overseers, the names of whom are known. Abel and Teyssandier came, morning and evening, to feed the cats with *pates* fashioned of the white meat of chicken. At his death Richelieu left a pension for his cats and to Abel and Teyssandier so that they might continue to care for their charges. When he died Richelieu left fourteen cats of which the names were: Mounard le Fouguex, Soumise, Serpolet, Gazette, Ludovic le Cruel, Mimie Piaillon, Felimare, Lucifer, Lodoiska, Rubis sur l'Ongle, Pyrame, Thisbe, Racan, and Perruque. These last two received their names from the fact that they were born in the wig of Racan, the academician.

Alexandre Landrin
*Le Chat*, 1894

RICHELIEU'S CATS
*Drawing by Peter DeSeve.*

# S

**SAM, fictional character; black; created by English writer Walter de la Mare (1873–1956); first appeared in short story "Broomsticks."**

Sam, according to de la Mare's haunting short story, is "what is called an 'intelligent' cat." He belongs to Miss Chauncey, a sixty-year-old spinster who lives in an ugly house on a lonely moor. Sam and Miss Chauncey get along fine until Sam begins to assert his independence by making mysterious nightly forays into the surrounding countryside. Sam, it turns out, has a secret life that ultimately leads Miss Chauncey to sell her house and move far away.

Sam had always been a fine upstanding creature, his fur jet-black and silky, his eyes a lambent green, even in sunshine, and at night a-glow like green topazes. He was now full seven years of age, and had an unusually powerful miaou. Living as he did quite alone with Miss Chauncey at Post Houses, it was natural that he should become her constant companion. For Post Houses was a singularly solitary house, standing almost in the middle of Haggurdsdon Moor, just where two wandering byways cross each other like the half-closed blades of a pair of shears or scissors.

. . . Like others of his kind. . . Sam delighted to lie in the window and idly watch the birds in the apple trees—tits and bullfinches and dunnocks—or to crouch over a mouse-hole for hours together. Such were his amusements (for he never ate his mice) while Miss Chauncey with cap and broom, duster and dishclout, went about her housework.

SAM

But he also had a way of examining things in which cats are not generally interested. He as good as told Miss Chauncey one afternoon that a hole was coming in her parlour carpet. For he walked to and fro and back and forth with his tail up, until she attended to him. And he certainly warned her, with a yelp like an Amazonian monkey, when a red-hot coal had set her kitchen mat on fire.

He would lie or sit with his whiskers to the North before noonday, and due South afterwards. In general his manners were perfection. But occasionally when she called him, his face would appear to knot itself into a frown—at any rate to assume a low sullen look, as if he expostulated "Why must you be interrupting me, Madam, when I am thinking of something else?" And now and then, Miss Chauncey fancied he would deliberately secrete himself or steal out and in of Post Houses unbeknown.

Walter de la Mare
"Broomsticks"

*A SEARLE CAT*
*"They're all against me"*

**SEARLE'S CATS; created by English artist Ronald Searle; appeared in, among other places, *Searle's Cats*.**

**SELIMA, pet and literary character; tortoise-shell tabby owned by English man of letters Horace Walpole (1717–97); drowned in a goldfish bowl while trying to catch a meal, thus offering proof of proverb "Curiosity killed the cat"; immortalized in a poem by English poet Thomas Gray (1716–71) sent to Walpole in a letter.**

'Twas on a lofty vase's side
   Where China's gayest art had dyed
   The azure flowers, that blow;
Demurest of the tabby kind,
The pensive Selima, reclined,
   Gazed on the lake below.

Her conscious tail her joy declared;
The fair round face, the snowy beard,
   The velvet of her paws,

*Circus cat secretly rehearsing Hamlet.*

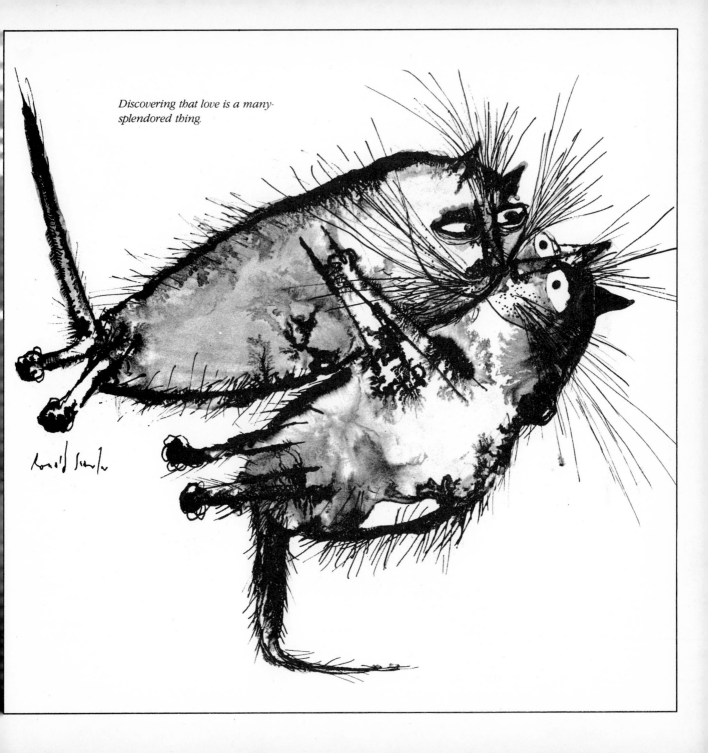

*Discovering that love is a many-splendored thing.*

Her coat, that with the tortoise vies,
Her ears of jet, and emerald eyes,
　　She saw; and purr'd applause.

Still had she gazed; but 'midst the tide
Two angel forms were seen to glide,
　　The genii of the stream:
Their scaly armour's Tyrian hue
Through richest purple to the view
　　Betray'd a golden gleam.

SELIMA

The hapless nymph with wonder saw:
A whisker first, and then a claw,
　　With many an ardent wish,
She stretch'd, in vain, to reach the prize.
What female heart can gold despise?
　　What cat's averse to fish?

Presumptuous maid! with looks intent
Again she stretch'd, again she bent,
　　Nor knew the gulf between.
(Malignant Fate sat by, and smiled)
The slipp'ry verge her feet beguiled,
　　She tumbled headlong in.

Eight times emerging from the flood
She mew'd to ev'ry wat'ry God,
　　Some speedy aid to send.
No Dolphin came, no Nereid stirr'd:
Nor cruel Tom, nor Susan heard.
　　A fav'rite has no friend!

From hence, ye beauties, undeceived,
Know, one false step is ne'er retrieved,
　　And be with caution bold.
Not all that tempts your wand'ring eyes
And heedless hearts is lawful prize.
　　Nor all that glitters, gold.

　　　　　　Thomas Gray
　　　　　　"Ode on the Death of a Favorite Cat
　　　　　　Drowned in a Tub of Gold Fishes"

**SHAN, First Feline of the Gerald Ford administration; Siamese; belonged to Susan Ford, President Ford's daughter.**

Shan has a thing about men. It hates all but one man, the president. It rubs up against the president's feet and, Susan said, hops onto Ford's lap and allows him to pet it. But no other male, not even Secretary of State Henry A. Kissinger, has established any more of a detente with Shan than has Liberty [President Ford's golden retriever].

Richard H. Growald
United Press International

SHAN
*Susan Ford's White House companion.*

**SIMPKIN, fictional character; created by Beatrix Potter (1866-1943); first appeared in *The Tailor of Gloucester* (1903), written and illustrated by Miss Potter; see also GINGER and TOM KITTEN.**

**SLIPPERS, White House pet during Theodore Roosevelt administration; gray; distinguished for having extra toes (polydactylism); see also TOM QUARTZ.**

[Slippers] always knew when it was time to put in an appearance at a big diplomatic dinner. On one historic occasion, the entire impressive procession of ambassadors, plenipotentiaries, and ministers had to be rerouted around the centre of the carpet—where Slippers was rolling luxuriously.

Fernand Mery
The Life, History and Magic of the Cat

**SPOOKY, comic-strip character; black with white paws and bandaged tail; created by Bill Holman (1903-    ); last appeared in mid-1950s.**

SPOOKY

**STEINLEN'S CATS**; created by French artist Theophile-Alexandre Steinlen (1859-1923); appeared in several books, including *Cats and Other Animals* (1933), *Cats: Wordless Picture-Stories* (undated) and *Steinlen Cats* (1980).

**SYLVESTER**<sup>TM</sup>, animated-cartoon character; created by I. "Friz" Freleng (1906-      ) first appeared in "Life With Feathers," television cartoon, March 24, 1945; appeared in motion picture, "Friz Freleng's Looney Looney Looney Bugs Bunny Movie" (1981); selected to serve as pitchman for 9-Lives Dry Cat Food (1981), making him a cousin-in-commerce to Morris the Cat; archrival: Tweety Bird, a canary with a speech impediment who always manages to get the better of his feline antagonist.

Sylvester's voice was done by Mel Blanc, who also did Daffy Duck's voice. The difference, though, is that for Daffy, Mel's voice is speeded up, while Sylvester's is a normal recording.

Like most of our villains, Sylvester is a loser but also a very determined character who never gives up. I think that's the reason he's funny. He just practically *destroys* himself in trying to get at Tweety Bird.

> "Friz" Freleng
> Creator

SYLVESTER AND TWEETY BIRD

# T

**TABBY**, First Feline of the Abraham Lincoln administration; belonged to Tad Lincoln, President Lincoln's son.

**TARAWOOD ANTIGONE**, pet and record holder; brown Burmese; owned by Mrs. Valerie Gane of England; gave birth to largest litter ever, nineteen kittens, on August 7, 1970: one female, fourteen males, four stillborn.

**THAT DARN CAT**, fictional character; portrayed by **SYN CAT**; star of Walt Disney film of the same name (1964); appeared with Dean Jones, Hayley Mills, Roddy McDowall, Frank Gorshin, William Demarest, and others in this comedy about a cat who became involved first in a bank robbery, and later in a full-fledged international intrigue.

**THOMASINA, fictional character; created by Paul Gallico; first appeared in *Thomasina: The Cat Who Thought She Was God* (New York, 1957;) also appeared in *The Three Lives of Thomasina*, co-starring Patrick McGoohan and Susan Hampshire (Walt Disney Productions, 1963).**

**TIGER, pet and record holder; long-haired part-Persian; ten years old; belongs to Mrs. Phyllis Dacey of England; heaviest cat on record; weight, forty-three pounds.**

**TIMMIE, pet; belonged to Bascom Timmons, Washington journalist, 1920s; chiefly noted for being in love with President Calvin Coolidge's pet canary.**

**TOBERMORY, fictional character; created by English writer Saki (pseudonym of H.H. Munro, 1870–1916); first appeared in *The Chronicles of Clovis* (1911).**

Tobermory is a talking cat (trained by Mr. Cornelius Appin, a weekend house guest of Lady Blemley's) who sets the Blemley household in a turmoil by speaking truthfully about the foibles and infidelities of the humans who inhabit it. Tobermory's acid tongue so infuriates his keepers that they conspire to murder him by putting poison in his food. He escapes that fate, although he meets a possibly worse one later on. Lesson: if cats could talk, their owners would be in trouble—and so, ultimately, would cats.

"And do you really ask us to believe," Sir Wilfrid was saying, "that you have discovered a means for instructing animals in the art of human speech, and that dear old Tobermory has proved your first successful pupil?"

"It is a project at which I have worked for the last seventeen years," said Mr. Appin, "but only during the last eight or nine months have I been rewarded with the glimmerings of success. Of course I have experimented with thousands of animals, but latterly only with cats, those wonderful creatures which have assimilated themselves so marvellously with our civilization while retaining all their highly

CALVIN COOLIDGE
*Unlikely cat lover.*

TIGER
*Fattest cat on record, shown in* Guinness Book of World Records, *editor Norris McWhirter.*

developed feral instincts. Here and there among cats one comes across an outstanding superior intellect, just as one does among the ruck of human beings, and when I made the acquaintance of Tobermory a week ago I saw at once that I was in contact with a 'Beyond-cat' of extraordinary intelligence. I had gone far along the road to success in recent experiments; with Tobermory, as you call him, I have reached the goal."

Mr. Appin concluded his remarkable statement in a voice which he strove to divest of a triumphant inflection. No one said "Rats," though Clovis's lips moved in a monosyllabic contortion which probably invoked those rodents of disbelief.

"And do you mean to say," asked Miss Resker, after a slight pause, "that you have taught Tobermory to say and understand easy sentences of one syllable?"

"My dear Miss Resker," said the wonder-worker patiently, "one teaches little children and savages and backward adults in that piecemeal fashion; when one has once solved the problem of making a beginning with an animal of highly developed intelligence one has no need for those halting methods. Tobermory can speak our language with perfect correctness."

This time Clovis very distinctly said, "Beyond-rats!" Sir Wilfrid was more polite, but equally skeptical.

"Hadn't we better have the cat in and judge for ourselves?" suggested Lady Blemley.

Sir Wilfrid went in search of the animal, and the company settled themselves down to the languid expectation of witnessing some more or less adroit drawing-room ventriloquism.

In a minute Sir Wilfrid was back in the room, his face white beneath its tan and his eyes dilated with excitement.

"By Gad, it's true!"

His agitation was unmistakably genuine, and his hearers started forward in a thrill of awakened interest.

Collapsing into an armchair he continued breathlessly: "I found him dozing in the smoking-room, and called out to him to come for his tea. He blinked at me in his usual way, and I said, 'Come on, Toby; don't keep us waiting'; and, by Gad! he drawled out in a most horribly natural voice that he'd come when he dashed well pleased! I nearly jumped out of my skin!"

Appin had preached to absolutely incredulous hearers; Sir Wilfrid's statement carried instant conviction. A Babel-like chorus of startled exclamation arose, amid which the scientist sat mutely enjoying the first fruit of his stupendous discovery.

In the midst of the clamour Tobermory entered the room and made his way with velvet tread and studied unconcern across to the group seated round the tea-table.

A sudden hush of awkwardness and constraint fell on the company. Somehow there seemed an element of embarrassment in addressing on equal terms of domestic cat of acknowledged mental ability.

"Will you have some milk, Tobermory?" asked Lady Blemley in a rather strained voice.

"I don't mind if I do," was the response, couched in a tone of even indifference. A shiver of suppressed excitement went through the

*TOBERMORY*

105

listeners, and Lady Blemley might be excused for pouring out the saucerful of milk rather unsteadily.

"I'm afraid I've spilt a good deal of it," she said apologetically.

"After all, it's not my Axminster," was Tobermory's rejoinder.

> Saki
> "Tobermory"

**TOM, animated-cartoon and comic-book character ("Tom and Jerry"); created by Fred Quimby, William Hanna, Joseph Barbera, 1939; first cartoon appearance, "Puss Gets the Boot," 1939; winner of seven Oscars; chief occupations, food gathering and unsuccessful mouse hunting.**

Joe and I developed the character in 1939. We were looking for something with a natural conflict, so that we would be able to keep the thing moving from one story to the next. What we came up with was the cat and mouse. The basic theme was that the bad guy always gets it, which he always did. We worked on "Tom and Jerry" for twenty years. People always seemed to enjoy it. It was a rough, slap-stick kind of humor, but it seemed to work very well.

> William Hanna
> Co-creator

**TOM KITTEN, fictional character; created by Beatrix Potter (1866–1943); first appeared in *The Tale of Tom Kitten* (1907), written and illustrated by Miss Potter; son of Mrs. Tabitha Twitchet; brother of Mittens and Moppet; best known for mischievousness and disinclination to wear clothes; see also GINGER and SIMPKIN.**

Once upon a time there were three little kittens, and their names were Mittens, Tom Kitten, and Moppet.

They had dear little fur coats of their own; and they tumbled about the doorstep and played in the dust.

But one day their mother—Mrs. Tabitha Twitchet—expected friends to tea; so she fetched the kittens indoors, to wash and dress them, before the fine company arrived.

First she scrubbed their faces. . . .

Then she combed their tails and whiskers. . . .

Then she brushed their fur. . . .

Tom was very naughty, and he scratched.

Mrs. Tabitha dressed Moppet and Mittens in clean pinafores and tuckers; and then she took all sorts of elegant uncomfortable clothes out of a chest of drawers, in order to dress up her son Thomas.

Tom Kitten was very fat, and he had grown; several buttons burst off. His mother sewed them on again.

When the three kittens were ready, Mrs. Tabitha unwisely turned them out into the garden, to be out of the way while she made hot buttered toast.

"Now you keep your frocks clean, children! You must walk on your hind legs. Keep away from the dirty ash-pit, and from Sally Henny Penny, and from the pig-stye and the Puddle-Ducks."

Moppet and Mittens walked down the garden path unsteadily. Presently they trod upon their pinafores and fell on their noses.

When they stood up there were several green smears!

"Let us climb up the rockery, and sit on the garden wall," said Moppet.

They turned their pinafores back to front, and went up with a skip and a jump; Moppet's white tucker fell down into the road.

Tom Kitten was quite unable to jump when walking upon his hind legs in trousers. He came up the rockery by degrees, breaking the ferns, and shedding buttons left and right.

He was all in pieces when he reached the top of the wall.

Moppet and Mittens tried to pull him together; his hat fell off, and the rest of his buttons burst.

While they were in difficulties, there was a pit pat paddle pat! and the three Puddle-Ducks came along the hard high road, marching one behind the other and doing the goose step—pit pat paddle pat! pit pat waddle pat!

They stopped and stood in a row, and stared up at the kittens. They had very small eyes and looked surpised.

Then the two duck-birds, Rebeccah and Jemima Puddle-Duck, picked up the hat and tucker and put them on.

Mittens laughed so that she fell off the wall. Moppet and Tom descended after her; the pinafores and all the rest of Tom's clothes came off on the way down.

"Come! Mr. Drake Puddle-Duck," said Moppet—"Come and help us to dress him! Come and button up Tom!"

Mr. Drake Puddle-Duck advanced in a slow sideways manner, and picked up the various articles.

But he put them on *himself!* They fitted him even worse than Tom Kitten.

"It's a very fine morning!" said Mr. Drake Puddle-Duck.

And he and Jemima and Rebeccah Puddle-Duck set off up the road, keeping step—pit pat, paddle pat! pit pat, waddle pat!

Then Tabitha Twitchit came down the garden and found her kittens on the wall with no clothes on.

She pulled them off the wall, smacked them, and took them back to the house.

"My friends will arrive in a minute, and you are not fit to be seen; I am affronted," said Mrs. Tabitha Twitchit.

She sent them upstairs; and I am sorry to say she told her friends that they were in bed with the measles; which was not true.

Quite the contrary; they were not in bed: *not* in the least.

Somehow there were very extraordinary noises over-head, which disturbed the dignity and repose of the tea party.

And I think that some day I shall have to make another, larger, book, to tell you more about Tom Kitten!

As for the Puddle-Ducks—they went into a pond.

The clothes all came off directly, because there were no buttons.

And Mr. Drake Puddle-Duck, and Jemima and Rebeccah, have been looking for them ever since.

> Beatrix Potter
> *The Tale of Tom Kitten*

**TOM KITTEN, pet; First Feline of the Kennedy administration; belonged to Caroline Kennedy, daughter of the president; first White House cat since SLIPPERS (Teddy Roosevelt, 1906); died August 21, 1962.**

Unlike many humans in the same position, he never wrote hs memoirs of his days in the White House and never discussed them for quotation, though he was privy to many official secrets.

> Obituary
> Alexandria (Va.) *Gazette*
> August 22, 1962

*Caroline and John-John in full Halloween regalia with friends in Oval Office.*

**TOM POES, Dutch comic-strip character; white tom; created by Marten Toonder (1912-    ); first appearance, 1938; name means "Tom Puss."**

**TOM QUARTZ, fictional character; gray tom; created by Mark Twain (pseudonym of Samuel Langhorne Clemens, 1835-1910); first described in Twain's novel *Roughing It* (first published 1872); preferred gold prospecting to rat catching and developed a profound dislike for quartz mining; see also TWAIN'S CATS and CATASAUQUA.**

I heard him talking about this animal once. He said:

"Gentlemen, I used to have a cat here, by the name of Tom Quartz, which you'd 'a' took an interest in, I reckon—most anybody would. I had him here eight year—and he was the remarkablest cat *I* ever see. He was a large gray one of the Tom specie, an' he had more hard, natchral sense than any man in this camp—'n' a *power* of dignity—he wouldn't let the Gov'ner of Californy be familiar with him. He never ketched a rat in his life—'peared to be above it. He never cared for nothing but mining. He knowed more about mining, that cat did, than any man *I* ever, ever see. You couldn't tell *him* noth'n' 'bout placer-diggin's—'n' as for pocket-mining, why he was just born for it. He would dig out after me an' Jim when we went over the hills prospect'n', and he would trot along behind us for as much as five mile, if we went so fur. An' he had the best judgment about mining-ground—why you never see anything like it. When we went to work he'd scatter a glance around, 'n' if he didn't think much of the indications, he would give a look as much as to say, 'Well, I'll have to get you to excuse *me*,' 'n' without another word he'd hyste his nose into the air 'n'. shove for home. But if the ground suited him, he would lay low 'n' keep dark till the first pan was washed, 'n' then he would sidle up 'n' take a look, an' if there was about six or seven grains of gold *he* was satisfied—he didn't want no better prospect 'n' that—'n' then he would lay down on our coats and snore like a steamboat till we'd struck the pocket, an' then get up 'n' superintend. He was nearly lightnin' on superintending."

Mark Twain
*Roughing It*

TOM POES

TOM QUARTZ
*Drawing by Peter DeSeve.*

**TOM QUARTZ, First Feline of the Theodore Roosevelt administration; named after cat described by Mark Twain in *Roughing It* (see previous entry); see also SLIPPERS.**

Tom Quartz is certainly the cunningest kitten I have ever seen. He is always playing pranks on Jack and I get very nervous lest Jack should grow too irritated. The other evening they were both in the library—Jack sleeping before the fire—Tom Quartz scampering about, an exceedingly playful little creature—which is about what he is. He would race across the floor, then jump upon the curtain or play with the tassle. Suddenly he spied Jack and galloped to him. Jack, looking exceedingly sullen and shame-faced, jumped out of the way and got upon the sofa and around the table, and Tom Quartz instantly jumped upon him again. Jack suddenly shifted to the other sofa, where Tom Quartz again went after him. Then Jack started for the door, while Tom made a rapid turn under the sofa and around the table and just as Jack reached the door leaped on his hind-quarters. Jack bounded forward and away and the two went tandem out of the room—Jack not co-operating at all; and about five minutes afterwards Tom Quartz stalked solemnly back.

Theodore Roosevelt
letter to son Kermit, January 6, 1903

**TONTO, fictional character; large ginger tabby "with eyes the color of marrons glaces"; created by Josh Greenfield and Paul Mazursky in *Harry and Tonto* (New York, 1973); later made into a movie starring Art Carney.**

Harry scoured through the bushes again, on hands and knees. In that position he remembered boyhood searches for lost baseballs and for a moment forgot what he was actually looking for. "Tonto" he called out urgently. He lifted his head and saw birds circling above. Even as he wondered if they might be vultures the birds passed on. He whistled twice for Tonto, thought for a moment he saw him peeking his head out from behind one of the gray tombstones that lined the ridge in the near distance like so many gray fallen sentries. He strained his eyes in that direction but there was no other sign of Tonto. Harry heard a rustling, a sound of movement in the bramble. Still whistling, he crept out of the

bushes, backing onto the gravel at the side of the road. And rising, dusting himself, turned around.

There was Tonto, nonchalantly licking himself. Very contented.

Harry was furious. "I don't like it!" he shouted. "I don't like it one bit! You rotten cat. You half scared the life out of me. I tell you, Tonto, I don't like your attitude."

Harry kneeled down. The cat was purring. Harry found the leash in his coat pocket and snapped it on. He rubbed Tonto's head and smiled. How could he stay angry with Tonto for very long? He nuzzled his own head into Tonto's fur.

"You don't like those buses, do you?" He moved his own head back and forth. "You want to be free, don't you?"

Tonto purred louder. Harry rose and picked up his Gladstone. He looked around for Tonto's case. He had left it on the bus. "Well," he turned to the cat, "that's show business."

And together they began to walk down the road.

## TOP CAT, animated-cartoon character and television personality; first appeared on *Top Cat,* prime-time animated cartoon (ABC, 1961); character based on Sergeant Bilko; voice by Arnold Stang; best friend, "Benny the Ball."

## TOUGH TOM, fictional character; created by Paul Gallico (1897–1976); first appeared in "The Ballad of Tough Tom."

That's right!
Those are tufts of my fur you're looking at.
What about it?
You don't see the other cat, do you?
What are a few hairs
Compared to an ear?
I didn't get the whole of his off
Because by then he was already heading south,
Having had enough.
But it was eminently satisfactory.
My name is Tough Tom,
And I am King of the Car Park.

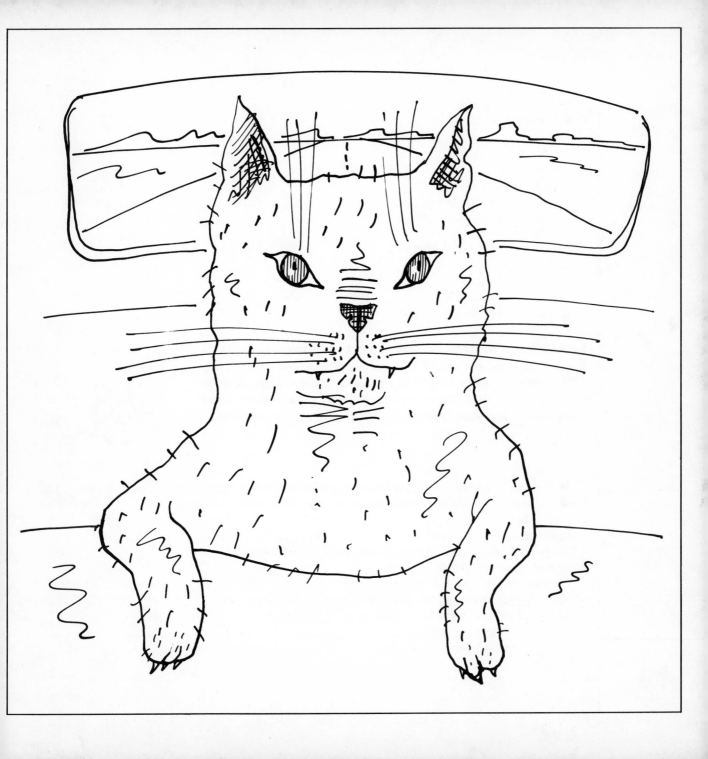

When the sun shines
It warms the hoods of the cars for us.
We like that.
We lie on them.
Sometimes we get chased because
We leave footmarks on the cars,
But most of the time nobody bothers,
We have our own crowd that comes here
To sun.
But I say who does and who doesn't.
See?
Because I'm King of the Car Park.
                    Paul Gallico
                    "The Ballad of Tough Tom"

**TWAIN'S CATS; pets, numerous cats belonging to Mark Twain (pseudonym of Samuel Langhorne Clemens, 1835-1910), including Apollinaris, Beelzebub, Blatherskite, Buffalo Bill, Sour Mash, Tammany, and Zoroaster; see also TOM QUARTZ and CATASAUQUA.**

Redding Connecticut,
Oct. 2, 08.

Dear Mrs. Patterson,—The contents of your letter are very pleasant and very welcome, and I thank you for them, sincerely. If I can find a photograph of my "Tammany" and her kittens, I will enclose it in this. One of them likes to be crammed into a corner-pocket of the billiard table—which he fits as snugly as does a finger in a glove and then he watches the game (and obstructs it) by the hour, and spoils many a shot by putting out his paw and changing the direction of a passing ball. Whenever a ball is in his arms, or so close to him that it cannot be played upon with risk of hurting him, the player is privileged to remove it to anyone of the 3 spots that chances to be vacant....

                    Sincerely yours,
                    S.L. Clemens

TWAIN'S CATS
*A drawing by the author (above) and the author himself (right).*

# V

**THE VAMPIRE CAT OF NABESHIMA, legendary figure from Japanese folklore, described in A.B. Mitford's *Tales of Old Japan*.**

This legend tells of a demon cat who kills Otoyo, a lovely maiden, by biting her on the neck and sucking out her blood, then buries the corpse and assumes the identity of the young woman. She proceeds to bewitch the prince who had been in love with Otoyo, visiting him nightly to extract his vital essence, gradually bringing him to the point of death. The prince's chief advisor, determined to discover the source of his master's sickness, sets guards to watch him as he sleeps. But they become mysteriously drowsy at their posts, finally falling asleep and allowing the goblin cat access to the prince as he lies there helpless. As a last resort, the chief advisor stands watch himself, cutting himself on the leg so that the pain will keep him awake. The cat/woman cannot bewitch him, and so flees to the mountains where she is finally hunted down and killed.

# W

**WEBSTER, fictional character; black; created by English writer P.G. Wodehouse (1881-1975); first appeared in *Mulliner Nights;* owned by Theodore Bongo-Bongo, wealthy uncle of an artist named Lancelot; has such an aristocratic bearing that he makes humans in his presence feel tactless and uncomfortable.**

Webster was very large and very black and very composed. He conveyed the impression of being a cat of deep reserves. Descendant of a long line of ecclesiastical ancestors who had conducted their decorous courtships beneath the shadow of cathedrals and on the back walls of bishops' palaces, he had that exquisite poise which one sees in high dignitaries of the Church. His eyes were clear and steady, and seemed to pierce to the very roots of the young man's soul, filling him with a sense of guilt.

Once, long ago, in his hot childhood, Lancelot, spending his summer holidays at the Deanery, had been so far carried away by ginger-beer and original sin as to plug a senior canon in the leg with his air gun—only to discover, on turning, that a visiting archdeacon had been a spectator of the entire incident from his immediate rear. As he felt then, when meeting the archdeacon's eye, so did he feel now as Webster's gaze played silently upon him.

> P.G. Wodehouse
> "The Story of Webster"

WEBSTER

**WHITE CAT, trademark and company mascot; appeared on logo of a Philadelphia tobacco company in the early 1900's.**

**WHITE HEATHER, pet; belonged to Queen Victoria of England (1819-1901); home, Buckingham Palace; survived Victoria's death and was taken up by her successor, King Edward VII.**

**WILLIAMINA, pet; belonged to English novelist Charles Dickens (1812-70); originally named WILLIAM; renamed after giving birth to a litter of kittens; pestered Dickens by putting out his candle when he was reading.**

*right:*
QUEEN VICTORIA AND
WHITE HEATHER
*A cat with royal blood.*

TEXT ACKNOWLEDGMENTS

We gratefully acknowledge permission to reprint the following copyrighted material.

**P. 6,** From AESOP'S FABLES. Illustrated Library Edition, 1947. Used by permission of Grosset & Dunlap, Inc.

**P. 9,** THE TIGER IN THE HOUSE by Carl Van Vechten. Alfred A. Knopf, Inc.

**P. 10,** Bastet. THE LIFE, HISTORY AND MAGIC OF THE CAT by Fernand Mery. Copyright, Editions, Robert Laffont, Paris.

**P. 19,** From THE CAT IN THE HAT by Dr. Seuss. Copyright © 1957 by Dr. Seuss. Reprinted by permission of Random House, Inc.

**P. 26,** CHESSIE. Copyright © 1936, 1963 by Ruth Carroll. Reprinted by permission of Julian Messner, a Simon and Schuster division of Gulf & Western Corporation.

**P. 28,** Reprinted by permission of Farrar, Straus and Giroux, Inc. Selection from THE CAT by Colette, translated by Antonia White. Copyright 1955 by Farrar, Straus and Cudahy, Inc. (now Farrar, Straus and Giroux, Inc.)

**P. 36,** THE TIGER IN THE HOUSE by Carl Van Vechten, Alfred A. Knopf, 1920.

**P. 37,** THE LIFE, HISTORY AND MAGIC OF THE CAT, by Fernand Mery. Copyright, Editions Robert Laffont, Paris.

**P. 44,** Excerpt from PENROD AND SAM by Booth Tarkington. Copyright 1916 by Doubleday & Company, Inc. Reprinted by permission of Doubleday & Company, Inc.

**P. 46,** Excerpted from the book ALGONQUIN CAT, a story by Val Schaffner. Copyright © 1980 by Val Schaffner. Reprinted by permission of Delacorte Press/ Eleanor Friede.

**P. 50,** PAPA HEMINGWAY. Copyright © 1955, 1959, 1966, by A.E. Hotchner. Used by permission of International Creative Management.

**P. 52,** From THE ABANDONED, by Paul Gallico. Copyright 1950 by Paul Gallico. Reprinted by permission of Alfred A. Knopf, Inc.

**P. 54,** THE LIFE, HISTORY AND MAGIC OF THE CAT by Fernand Mery. Copyright, Editions Robert Laffont, Paris.

**P. 58,** Reprinted from KRAZY KAT by George Herriman. Copyright © by permission of Grosset & Dunlap, Inc.

**P. 51,** Excerpt from THE LIFE AND TIMES OF ARCHY & MEHITABEL by Don Marquis. Copyright 1927, 1930, 1933, 1935 by Doubleday & Company, Inc. Copyright 1922, 1923, 1924, 1925, 1934 by P.F. Collier & Son Company. Copyright 1928, 1932, 1933 by Don Marquis. Reprinted by permission of Doubleday & Company, Inc.

**P. 66,** Minnaloushe. Reprinted with permission of Macmillan Publishing Co., Inc. from COLLECTED POEMS by William Butler Yeats. Copyright 1919 by Macmillan Publishing Co., Inc. renewed 1947 by Bertha Georgia Yeats.

**P. 72, 3,** Excerpt from ANNE FRANK: THE DIARY OF A YOUNG GIRL by Anne Frank. Copyright 1952 by Otto H. Frank. Reprinted by permission of Doubleday & Company, Inc.

**P. 74,** Tennessee Williams, ONE ARM and OTHER STORIES. Copyright 1948, 1954 by Tennessee Williams. Reprinted by permission of New Directions.

**P. 76,** SELECTED LETTERS OF H.P. LOVECRAFT. Reprinted by permission of Arkham House Publishers, Inc. Sauk City, Wisconsin 53583.

**P. 78,** NOT SO DUMB by Raymond Lee. Castle Books.

**P. 13,** Drawing by Booth; © 1978. The New Yorker Magazine, Inc.

**P. 14,** Photograph by Bill Hayward.

**P. 15,** Woodcut courtesy Fritz Eichenberg, © Heritage Press.

**P. 17,** Union Tribune Publishing Co. Publishers of the San Diego Union and Evening Star.

**P. 19,** From THE CAT IN THE HAT, by Dr. Seuss. Copyright © 1957 by Dr. Seuss. Reprinted by permission of Random House, Inc.

**P. 20,** New York Public Library Picture Collection.

**P. 21,** Drawing by Rudyard Kipling.

**P. 26,** Chessie System Railroads.

**P. 27,** CHESSIE, Copyright © 1936, 1963 by Ruth Carroll. Reprinted by permission of Julian Messner, a Simon & Schuster division of Gulf & Western Corporation.

**P. 29,** Photographer unknown.

**P. 31,** Photograph by Bill Hayward.

**P. 32,** New York Public Library Picture Collection.

**P. 33,** Keystone Press.

**P. 34,** Dusty. GUINNESS BOOK OF WORLD RECORDS © 1980 published by Sterling Publishing Company, 2 Park Avenue, New York, N.Y. 10016.

**P. 35,** New York Public Library Picture Collection.

**P. 37,** Felix The Cat Productions. From the Collection of Murray Tinkleman. Permission granted by King Features Syndicate, Inc.

**P. 39,** Reprinted with permission of Macmillan Publishing Co., Inc. from THE ADVENTURES OF PINOCCHIO by C. Collodi. Illustrations by Attilio Russino. First published in 1925.

**P. 40,** Drawing by Edward Lear.
S.K. Productions, Inc. Courtesy of Steve Krantz.

**P. 41,** Courtesy of Steve Krantz. The Museum of Modern Art Film Still Archive.

**P. 42-43,** GARFIELD © 1978, 1979. United Feature Syndicate, Inc.

**P. 45,** Photograph by Carl Fisher.
Drawing by Edward Gorey.

**P. 47,** Photograph by Bill Hayward.

**P. 48-49,** Courtesy of the McNaught Syndicate, Inc.

**P. 51,** Photograph by Peter Buckley.

**P. 53,** Drawing by Watteau.

**P. 54,** Drawing by Cocteau.

**P. 55,** From the Motion Picture ALIEN, courtesy of 20th Century Fox.

**P. 57,** Copyright © 1975 By Kliban; from CAT, Published by Workman Publishing Co., Inc. 1975.

**P. 58,** Photograph courtesy of King Features Syndicate, Inc.
Krazy Kat. King Features Syndicate Inc. From the collection of G.B. Trudeau.

**P. 59-60,** Krazy Kat. King Features Syndicate, Inc. From the collection of Murray Tinkleman.

**P. 63,** Drawing by George Herriman.

**P. 65,** Drawing by Peter de Seve.

**P. 67,** United Press International photo.

**P. 68-70,** Courtesy Star-Kist Foods, Inc.

As we said in the Introduction, we may have overlooked several of your favorite Great Cats. In any case, we would like to remedy that by providing the space below for your personal nominee. Greatness is, after all, in the eye of the beholder.